THOMAS COOK
Travellers

BELGIUM

BY
GEORGE McDONALD

Produced by AA Publishing

Written by George McDonald
Original photography by Alex Kouprianoff

Edited, designed and produced by AA Publishing.
Maps © The Automobile Association 1994, 1996

Distributed in the United Kingdom by AA Publishing,
Norfolk House, Priestley Road, Basingstoke,
Hampshire RG24 9NY.

The contents of this publication are believed correct at
the time of printing. Nevertheless, the publishers cannot
accept responsibility for any errors or omissions, or for
changes in the details given in this guide, or for the
consequences of any reliance on the information
provided by the same. Assessments of attractions, hotels,
restaurants and so forth are based upon the author's
own experience, and therefore descriptions given in this
guide necessarily contain an element of subjective
opinion which may not reflect the publisher's opinion or
dictate a reader's own experiences on another occasion.
**We have tried to ensure accuracy in this guide, but things do
change and we would be grateful if readers would advise us of any
inaccuracies they may encounter.**

A CIP catalogue record for this book is available from the British Library.

ISBN 0 7495 1344 6

Published by AA Publishing (a trading name of Automobile Association
Developments Limited, whose registered office is Norfolk House,
Priestley Road, Basingstoke, Hampshire RG24 9NY. Registered number
1878835) and the Thomas Cook Group Ltd.

Colour separation: BTB Colour Reproduction, Whitchurch, Hampshire.
Printed by Edicoes ASA, Oporto, Portugal

Front cover: *the Grand Place, Brussels,* Back cover: *market place, Bruges;
Zimmer Tower, Lier*; Title page: *Waterloo House, Antwerp*; Above: *Spa
poster* **Cover picture credits** AA Photo Library (A Kouprianoff):
Back cover bottom, Spine; Zefa Pictures Ltd: Front cover, Back
cover bottom

Contents

About this Book

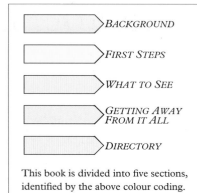

> BACKGROUND
>
> FIRST STEPS
>
> WHAT TO SEE
>
> GETTING AWAY FROM IT ALL
>
> DIRECTORY

This book is divided into five sections, identified by the above colour coding.

The **Background** gives an introduction to the country – its history, geography, politics, culture.

First Steps offers practical advice on arriving and getting around.

What to See is an alphabetical listing of places to visit, divided into three regions, interspersed with walks and tours.

Getting Away From it All highlights places off the beaten track where it's possible to relax and enjoy peace and quiet.

Finally, the **Directory** provides practical information – from shopping and entertainment to children and sport, including a section on business matters. Special highly illustrated **features** on specific aspects of the country appear throughout the book.

MAPPING
The maps in this book use international country symbols:
D Germany
F France
L Luxembourg
NL The Netherlands

Folklore parade in Bruges

BACKGROUND

'Of all the peoples of Gaul, the
Belgians are the bravest.'

JULIUS CAESAR
whose Roman legions invaded,
and finally conquered, the territory of
the Belgae between 58 and 54 BC.

Introduction

*I*t comes hard for a country if foreigners do not even know where it is. This has often been Belgium's fate, although two millennia of invaders somehow managed to find the way. The country's tourism authorities must, however, be patient with visitors who believe that Antwerpen (Antwerp) is a Dutch city, that Liège (Luik) is part of France, and that Bruxelles (Brussels) is a suburb of Amsterdam.

Belgium does not conjure up the kind of sharp-edged image that links Holland with windmills, Germany with efficiency and France with fine cooking. Why not? One answer is that Belgium is not a sharp-edged kind of country. It has a diversity of language, culture, history and tradition that does not fit easily into a glib definition.

A guide to Belgium has to imply, if not always to say: 'This is not very commonly appreciated, but did you know that ...?'

Did you know that a bewildering succession of empires have left the

BELGIUM

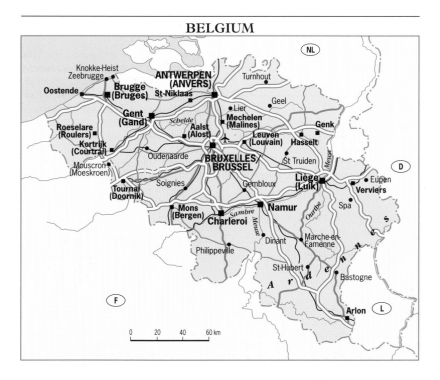

signature of their passing in countless monuments across the land; that Belgium has more than 400 kinds of beer, and 300 different cheeses; more Michelin star restaurants per capita than France; one of Europe's most extravagant Carnival traditions, and strongest economies; the only Michelangelo sculpture that was sold outside Italy ...?

Opening the book on Belgium is like finding a tiny jewel hidden beneath layers of obscurity. Belgians do not share the arrogance of some countries – that,

Two-thirds of a million begonias on display in the Grand-Place for Brussels' Carpet of Flowers

of course, their homeland is wonderful and visitors should count themselves privileged to experience it. Instead, they are often refreshingly surprised that a foreigner should take an interest in the little place they call home.

This guide aims to make the Belgians' job a little easier, by introducing visitors to the many and undoubted charms of this small country that have remained unheralded for so long. At the very least, it aims to clear up those popular misconceptions that abound about the nationality of Antwerp, Liège and Brussels and put these fine cities firmly in the country to which they belong.

History

Around 300BC
A Celtic tribe, the Belgae, occupy the territory that broadly corresponds to modern Belgium.

58–54BC
Julius Caesar conquers the Belgae. The Romans subsequently incorporate their territory into the Empire.

AD406 onwards
The Franks occupy Belgium, eventually locating their capital at Tournai.

496
Clovis, King of the Franks, converts to Christianity.

768
Charlemagne is crowned King of the Franks and in 800 becomes the first Holy Roman Emperor.

979
The Duke of Lorraine occupies a castle on the island of Saint-Géry in what is now Brussels. This is traditionally considered as the date of the city's foundation.

980
The Prince-Bishops of Liège acquire political power over their ecclesiastic domain.

12th century
The Flemish 'cloth towns' of Bruges, Ghent and Ypres begin to grow in wealth and influence.

1302
Battle of the Golden Spurs near Kortrijk: Flemish peasants slaughter the flower of French chivalry.

1419
Philip the Good, Duke of Burgundy, becomes Count of Flanders and gradually extends his domain to include most of Belgium, Holland and Luxembourg.

1468
Charles, Duke of Burgundy, annexes Liège.

1477
Duchess Marie of Burgundy marries the Hapsburg ruler of Austria, Maximilian. Low Countries pass to Hapsburg rule.

1516
Maximilian's grandson, Charles, of the Spanish branch of the Hapsburgs, becomes King of Spain and subsequently Holy Roman Emperor.

1517
The seeds of the Reformation, Protestantism and religious conflict in the Low Countries are sown with the publication of Martin Luther's Theses.

1555
Charles V abdicates in favour of his son Philip II, who imposes strict adherence to Catholicism by force.

1576
Pacification of Ghent guarantees freedom of religious belief, but differences arise between the Catholic south and Protestant north.

1579
Belgium elects to stay with Spain, while Holland forms an independent confederation.

1695
Bombardment of Brussels by a French army. Grand-Place is destroyed.

1713
The Treaty of Utrecht cedes the Low Countries to Austria.

1740–48
France invades and occupies Belgium. The Treaty of Aachen returns the country to Austria.

1789
The French Revolution. Brabant rises

up against the Austrians at Turnhout, expelling them temporarily.

1794
The French Republic annexes Belgium.

1815
Napoleon Bonaparte is defeated at Waterloo outside Brussels. Belgium is ceded to the Netherlands.

1830
The Belgians revolt against Dutch rule, and the War of Independence begins.

1831
Prince Leopold of Saxe-Coburg is crowned Leopold I, first King of the Belgians.

1835
The Continent's first railway is inaugurated, from Brussels to Mechelen.

1855
Belgium acquires a colonial empire in Africa, in the territory later known as the Belgian Congo (present-day Zaïre).

1914–18
World War I. Apart from a small area around Ypres and De Panne, Belgium is occupied by the Germans.

1934
Albert, the heroic Soldier King of World War I, dies in a climbing accident.

1940–44
Belgium is occupied by Nazi Germany during World War II.

1948
Benelux, a customs union between Belgium, the Netherlands and Luxembourg, is instituted, later becoming an economic union.

1951
King Baudouin, the reigning King of the Belgians, ascends the throne.

1957
Belgium joins the European Economic Community, the Common Market.

1958
The World Fair at the Heysel.

Ambiorix, chief of the Belgae, at Tournai, where he defeated Julius Caesar's legions

1959
Commission of the European Community located in Brussels, which becomes *de facto* Capital of Europe.

1960
Independence of the Belgian Congo, which becomes Zaïre.

1967
NATO moves to Brussels from Paris.

1980
The 150th anniversary of Belgian independence.

1989
Reorganisation of the Belgian state. There are now three regions: Brussels Capital, Flanders and Wallonia.

1990
King Baudouin celebrates the 40th anniversary of his reign and the 160th anniversary of Belgian independence.

1993
King Baudouin dies. His brother takes the throne as King Albert II.

An Imperial Past

*B*elgium has often been a target of other nations' imperial ambitions. First on the scene were the Romans, led by Julius Caesar. He 'came, saw and conquered' the Belgae and their allies in 58BC although, by Caesar's own account, the Belgian tribes were among the toughest fighters he ever faced.

When the Romans pushed the Empire's frontier forward to the River Rhine, they left behind a peaceful backwater. Villas were established, strategic roads connected France with legionary bases on the Rhine, and towns like Tongeren and Tournai developed as centres of trade and government.

Rome's grip gradually weakened under the hammer-blows of barbarian incursions, and when the Rhine barrier was fatally breached in AD406 Roman control in Belgium and France came to an end.

The Franks

The torch of power passed to the hands of the Franks who, under King Pepin, turned out to be quite civilised, for barbarians. Establishing their capital at Tournai, they extended their rule over Belgium, France and parts of Germany and Holland.

With the accession of Charlemagne, born in Liège in 742 and crowned Holy Roman Emperor in 800, the Frankish Empire reached its zenith. Charlemagne died in 814 and the empire was later split in three, setting in train a process of disintegration.

In this division of the empire, Belgium was also divided: Flanders remained attached to France, while Wallonia went with Lorraine. In succeeding centuries, local overlords became more powerful, the Counts of Flanders dominating the north while the Dukes of Lorraine and the Prince-Bishops of Liège were prominent in the south.

One salient fact emerged from this turbulent period:

the regions and peoples that would one day form Belgium were squeezed between France and Germany. This was a dangerous position to occupy, as would become only too clear as the centuries progressed.

The Burgundians

Belgium's connection with Burgundy began in 1369, when Duke Philip of Burgundy married the Count of Flanders' daughter, inheriting both Belgium and Holland on the count's death in 1384.

A later duke, Philip the Good, added Namur in 1429, Brabant and Limburg in 1430, and Hainaut in 1433. Liège was added by his successor, Charles the Bold. Belgium was taking shape, especially as Philip the Good had established the duchy's capital in Brussels.

The Habsburgs

Mary of Burgundy, who inherited Charles the Bold's

Leopold II, King of the Belgians from 1865 to 1909

duchy, married Prince Maximilian of the Austrian Habsburg Empire, whose possessions included Spain, and in time this new empire took control. Under Charles V, the empire experienced a golden age and his reign is still recalled every year in the Ommegang (Procession), a stunningly colourful event in Brussels' Grand-Place commemorating Charles's entry into his capital in 1549.

Charles V was succeeded by Philip II, a fanatical Spanish Catholic who tried to crush Protestantism in the Low Countries, unleashing a wave of violence. The outcome of religious wars and succession disputes was that in 1713 Belgium was handed over to the Austrian branch of the Habsburgs.

Napoleon Bonaparte, whose imperial career came to an end at Waterloo in 1815

Napoleon

In 1795, a new round of imperial musical-chairs began when France invaded, Belgium later becoming part of the Napoleonic Empire. The last trumpet of Napoleon's grand imperial career was sounded in the year 1815 outside Brussels, near the village of Waterloo.

The era of other people's empires came to an end with Belgium's revolt from Dutch rule in 1830, except for two brief experiences of German occupation in the 20th century.

Today, a new kind of 'empire' is being forged, in the European Union. Its capital, for all practical purposes, is Brussels. Julius Caesar, Charlemagne, Philip the Good and Charles V would no doubt appreciate the vagaries of fortune that have led to such a state of affairs.

Geography

*W*ith a population of some 10 million living in 30,520sq km, Belgium is a small country with a population density of just under 330 persons per sq km, one of the world's highest. Its geographical structure almost exactly mirrors that of its language divide. Flanders has the coastline, while Wallonia, including its small German-speaking area, has its heartland in the glacier-sculpted hills and forests of the Ardennes.

Few countries are better placed to claim ownership of that greatly desired piece of real-estate known as the 'Heart of Europe'. The Channel Tunnel comes ashore close to the Belgian border, while some of Europe's most important road and rail links intersect at Brussels, Antwerp and Liège. These facts complement Brussels' role as 'Capital of Europe' and Antwerp's as Europe's second port (after Rotterdam).

Flanders

Physically, Flanders' geography ranges from the very low – below sea level – to the not-quite-so-low. Behind the sand-dunes and the man-made sea defences is the reclaimed land called *polders*, just like those of neighbouring Holland though not so extensive. If the sea defences were ever breached by a particularly severe North Sea storm, part of West Flanders would go under water.

Flanders' other important landscape is the Kempen, a moorland region along the border with Holland (see pages 76–7). Sparsely populated, it was long a difficult area to penetrate, and even today most major roads run around rather than through it.

Finally, since Wallonia has its Ardennes, it seems only fair that Flanders should have one also, and it has, the Vlaamse Ardennen (Flemish Ardennes). Located around Ronse and Geraardsbergen, the Flemish Ardennes are hilly and pretty enough but only a pale shadow of the original.

Wallonia

The real thing, in the area lying roughly between the River Meuse and the German border, is the eroded remnant of a mountain range worn down by glaciers, wind and rain (see pages 94–9). Dinosaur fossils have been found in the Ardennes and geologists make field-trips there in search of clues about glaciation.

From the residents' and tourists' point of view, such inexorable forces have created a landscape rich in agricultural and recreational possibilities. Forests, steep valleys and fast-flowing rivers mark the scenery with the distinctive signature of an outdoor paradise.

In the northern Ardennes, mostly in the German-speaking East Cantons, is the Hautes Fagnes (see page 102), a high plateau of ancient peat moors and bogs which had a habit of swallowing up unwary travellers who encountered bad weather while crossing it. Belgium's highest point is here, at the Signal de Botrange and at the less than dizzy altitude of 694m.

Brussels

Brussels, by contrast, grew over the low hills and swampy valleys of Brabant.

While Flanders' river, the Scheldt, and Wallonia's, the Meuse, flow proudly along beneath open skies, Brussels' river, the Senne, was forced underground during the last century to make way for grandiose urban development schemes.

Yet in the Forest of Soignes, an extensive wooded area south of the capital, Brussels has its own piece of rural charm and a nearby place of escape for citizens grown weary of life in Europe's fast lane.

Climate

Belgium's climate is temperate: it never gets too hot or too cold; never too wet or too dry. Summers tend to be warm, with

Many Belgians like nothing better than to be beside the seaside in Flanders

peak temperatures reaching into the high 30°s Celsius. Spring and autumn are cooler, more changeable, often blustery. Rain is a fact of life at any time.

PROVINCES/LANGUAGE AREAS

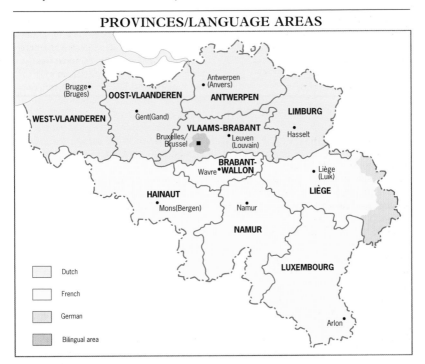

Politics

*F*or a country with a population of just 10 million, Belgium has given itself a political and governmental system that, in its level of complexity, would do justice to a far-flung empire.

The 1831 constitution established Belgium as a hereditary and constitutional monarchy. Originally a centralised state, important changes since World War II have led to a loosely federated one. There are two houses of Parliament: the Senate, with 71 members, including representatives of the 10 provinces (Antwerp, East Flanders, Flemish Brabant, Hainaut, Liège, Limburg, Luxembourg, Namur Walloon Brabant and West Flanders); and the Chamber of Representatives, with 150 members.

The changes have boosted the importance of Belgium's traditional regions and communities at the expense of the central government, which now basically retains power over defence, foreign policy, national economic policy and social security, while the regions have autonomy over their own affairs.

These regions are Flanders, Wallonia and Brussels Capital, while the mainly German-speaking East Cantons, though part of Wallonia, have powers similar to the regions. In addition to governments for these four political divisions, there are three councils which look after the cultural interests of the communities: Dutch, French and German.

One result of all this government is a bureaucracy which would stifle all individual initiative if Belgians were not so adept at ignoring or side-stepping it.

Political parties

The many and marvellous forms of Belgian government have led to a convoluted political system and this has been exacerbated by the growth of regional power. Ambitious politicians can climb to power via national or regional politics, and a tug of war is

The National Palace in Brussels, seat of Belgium's parliament

The late King Baudouin, a widely popular monarch, on a 'meet the people' exercise

under way between these two forces to determine which will predominate.

Compromise, however, is usually the name of the game. There are three main political groupings, representing the left, centre and right of the spectrum: Socialist, Christian Socialist and the Liberty and Reform Party. In addition, there are Communists, Ecologists, one Walloon and two Flemish nationalist parties: the Walloon Assembly, the Flemish Block and the People's Union. Proportional representation virtually guarantees that no single party controls Parliament, and coalitions are a way of life.

Politics is the art of the possible, and Belgian politicians (or some of them) have had to be supreme artists to balance not only the ideological forces, but also the regional ones. The latter dictate that each community pays more attention to advancing its own interests than to the good of the whole. Yet the system has survived because those interests are rarely pushed far enough to precipitate a crisis.

Conversely, the government seems to exist in a more or less permanent state of crisis. Thus are the tensions and contradictions of Belgian society mirrored in its governance, which is presumably how things should be in a democracy. This apparently stable form of instability may be threatened in future, not just by the growing powers of the regions, but by growing support for right-wing Flemish nationalists and Walloon Greens, although this may prove to be only a passing phase.

Society

The sound and fury emanating from the various stages of government does not mean that most Belgians behave in this way. On the contrary, they display a healthy scepticism towards politicians. Belgians prosper by ignoring the political powers-that-be most of the time, only paying them lip-service when it is advantageous to do so.

Who you know counts for much in a society where petty officialdom makes the most of its prerogatives. Everything from getting a telephone installed to acquiring a feather-bedded post in government service is made easier by having a friend in the right place. If the contact is a politician in favour, even if only temporarily, so much the better.

ROYAL FAMILY

King Albert II and (left) with Queen Paola

Belgium's is a relatively recent royal house. When an opera audience in Brussels got fired up by a patriotic aria in 1830, they set in train a revolution that led, the following year, to Prince Leopold of Saxe-Coburg being crowned King of the Belgians.

His reign (1831–65) was taken up with the struggle for independence from Holland, and then with the country's first confident steps as a nation. Belgium opened the Continent's first railway and took the industrial revolution in its stride.

Leopold was succeeded by his son, Leopold II (1865–1909), in whose reign Belgian cities were embellished with

grandiose monuments, and the Congo became a colony. Albert (1909–34) was the dashing 'Soldier King' of World War I, who led the Belgian army's resistance to German invasion. He died in a climbing accident in the Ardennes.

Leopold III had no such romantic legend. Surrendering to Hitler's invaders in 1940, he was suspected of collaboration, but also defended as having protected his people as best he could from Nazi tyranny. A post-war referendum showed a modest majority in favour of his return from exile, but he abdicated in 1951 in favour of his son, King Baudouin (1951–93).

Baudouin and his Spanish-born wife Queen Fabiola were unassuming and widely popular monarchs. Indeed, they were often seen as the 'glue' which held this fractious nation together. King Baudouin's reign was not without controversy, however, as when he briefly 'abdicated' to avoid signing an abortion Bill. His sudden death in 1993 precipitated widespread spontaneous mourning among ordinary Belgians of all communities, with his lying-in-state and funeral offering a platform for them to share his own dismay at politicians who had been trying to split the country.

Baudouin's brother, Prince Albert of Liège, succeeded as Albert II. His Italian-born wife Paola became queen.

Culture

*W*e may talk about 'German character', or 'English politeness', or 'French haughtiness', or 'Dutch sobriety' and, allowing for some variation, have a fair idea of what we mean. No such glib expression characterises the Belgians.

The key to Belgium's identity (or as some would say, lack of one) lies in the line that cuts clear across the country's middle, separating Dutch-speaking Flanders from French-speaking Wallonia. It marks Europe's millennia-old Great Divide: the linguistic and cultural frontier between the Germanic north and the Latin south.

Belgium deals with this divide, not as a matter of history or textbook study, but as a question of everyday life. It runs across fields and lakes, through communities and politics, over national ideals and the practical need for co-operation. It is a fracture-line seemingly awaiting only a tremor with the right force on the social Richter Scale to tear the country apart.

Yet rumours of Belgium's demise have been heard before and have always proved to be greatly exaggerated. When it came down to it, back in 1830, both communities preferred to go with each other in a common country than to diverge and entrust their fates to their neighbours. History had taught the Belgians that if they did not hang together, they would surely hang separately.

Tradition
Family and tradition still mean something here, and if tradition shows

A 'Brueghelian feast' maintains the tradition of over-indulgence in eating and drinking

up as pride in their Flemish or Walloon roots, it rarely manifests itself in personal animosity towards members of the other community. Belgians get along with each other far better than foreigners – or even they themselves – think.

A myth persists, nevertheless, that Belgians are somehow 'boring'. The myth is partly explained by Belgium's bigger neighbours, the 'exciting' French, Germans, Dutch and British, none of whom are noticeably reticent about blowing their own trumpet. The Belgians' apparent reluctance to blow theirs may have had sound justification in the past: whenever those neighbours, and others yet more distant, noticed Belgium they decided they liked it so much that they wanted it all for themselves.

Mass of contradictions

Belgian culture is rooted in contradictions and nourished by diversity. It is a deeply traditional society, but one which quietly aspires to be at the forefront (of the new Europe, for example). Government is bureaucratic enough to have warmed the heart of any Soviet *apparatchik*, and there are more laws than anyone knows what to do with, so people have learned to sidestep the first, ignore the second, and never allow their individuality to be submerged.

That diversity has its foundation in the Flanders/Wallonia background and takes concrete form in the dark, Spanish aspect of one Belgian compared with the blond, Nordic look of another. Both, however, may share the characteristic Burgundian look that Brueghel captured so well and that can still be seen, as if staring out of a centuries-old canvas, today.

This is a country that eats and drinks

A street artist grapples with capturing the intricacies of Brussels' Grand-Place

its way happily through the day, yet makes sure that the work (or at least most of it) gets done; where ordinary courtesies are ever-present beneath the formal surface; where bourgeois and Brueghelian values somehow co-exist peacefully – often within the same person.

'An enviable Burgundian lifestyle' is an oft-repeated shorthand for the Belgian way of life, but Belgium somehow manages to combine this with being the European Union's biggest per capita exporter, while the Belgian franc regularly occupies the top spot in the European Exchange Rate Mechanism. They are no slouches when it comes to earning the money that pays for their lifestyle.

Don't try to understand it; even the Belgians themselves can't. They just get on with living it.

GUILDS AND SOCIETIES

In almost every Belgian town stand centuries-old buildings inscribed with words like *brasseurs* and *bakkers* (brewers and bakers). These are the guild-houses, and their guildsmen were once a powerful force in Belgian society.

Trade guilds stood alongside noble bodies such as the Compagnie Royale des Anciens Arquebusiers (Royal Company of Old Musketeers) and the Schuttersgilden (Shooters' Guilds), whose members were handy with longbow, crossbow or musket. Such bodies still exist today, with strict membership requirements and arcane rituals.

Uniforms and costumes, ranging from the historically accurate to the weird and wonderful, are paraded throughout this tradition-minded land. Gastronomic *confréries* (brotherhoods) are commonplace, honouring the seemingly oddest things: the Confrérie Li Crochon d'Onhaye, for example, venerates an ancient dish which looks suspiciously like grilled cheese and ham on toast, while the Confrérie de la Tarte au Fromage takes its cue from La Blanke Doreye de Djodogne, a cheesecake peculiar to Jodoigne.

Others maintain traditions of fanfares, giant folkloric mannekins, harlequins, drinks, hunts, pâtés, carnivals, saints, dances and religious processions. Most momentous of all, is the blue-blooded society which annually puts on a kaleidoscopic procession, the Ommegang, recalling Emperor Charles V's triumphant entry into Brussels in 1549.

No cause is too humble, or too grand.

Showing the flag during the Ommegang, and youthful Gilles honouring Manneken-Pis

FIRST STEPS

'Our country has the unique advantage
of lying at the crossroads
of the great cultures of Europe.'
HIS ROYAL HIGHNESS, THE LATE KING
BAUDOUIN,
in a speech delivered in 1990 to mark his 60th birthday
and the 40th year of his reign.

French and Dutch share the space on Brussels' street signs

LANGUAGE

Language is usually the first problem that visitors to any foreign country encounter, and in Belgium language takes on a particular importance as it is the badge the country's communities wear on their sleeve to proclaim their distinct identity.

More foreign visitors to Belgium speak French than speak Dutch; some of them, travelling in Flanders, assume that by speaking French they are fitting in with at least part of Belgian culture. This might seem logical, but in Flanders they are likely to be asked if they wouldn't feel more comfortable speaking English instead.

Travellers in Wallonia are unlikely to find this problem, although Dutch speakers will occasionally run into blank walls in the French-speaking heartland. In any case, not many Belgians are so intent on establishing their own language's priority that they would translate this into bad manners towards visitors.

To the outside observer, the language 'thing' can be immensely entertaining. Conversations are often conducted in a linguistic no-man's-land of mixed French and Dutch sentences, sometimes with English thrown in for good measure. Almost all advertising is in the two languages. Both communities have their speciality dishes, beers and cheeses, proudly named in French or Flemish (as near as anything can be to Dutch). Government forms – before being filled-in in triplicate – must first be printed in two versions.

Three versions, when German is included. As if to add icing to the linguistic cake, there is a small German-speaking community in the East Cantons (see pages 100–5) part of Wallonia. Flanders has no equivalent minority, although some people in West Flanders speak a dialect that other Flemings have trouble understanding.

On the plus side, many Belgians speak English, particularly in Flanders but increasingly in Wallonia as well. German too is quite widely spoken.

TRAVELLING AROUND

The tourist infrastructure at national, regional, provincial, city, local and even village level is generally excellent. All are sources of maps, brochures, leaflets, magazines, guides, advice, accommodation information and reservations.

As always it is wise to explore off the beaten track, hoping for whatever serendipity may provide. Even around Brussels and Antwerp there are surprises to be found in small villages, old fortified farms, and distinctive landscapes. When this approach is adopted in the Ardennes, the Kempen, West Flanders, or the Botte (Boot) of Hainaut, the traveller will come across communities that seem isolated enough to be living in another world.

GETTING AROUND

This is a small country with excellent transport networks, particularly its all-illuminated motorway system. Brussels' ring road, however, is more a squashed oval than a ring, because of opposition from some communities to having tarmac poured across their gardens.

A couple of hours of vigorous driving will get you just about anywhere in Belgium, putting the Flemish art cities and the fresh-air Ardennes on each other's doorstep. Vigorous driving is what many Belgians believe in, combined with an apparent blindness to potential danger that contributes to some of western Europe's worst accident statistics.

The cities are no better. It has been well said that Belgians prefer to crash rather than give up their priority when joining traffic from the right, and a casual survey of the number of dented cars adds credence to this seemingly absurd idea. Drivers take their priority under any and all circumstances; the few timid ones who do not simply get their bashes in the rear.

Pedestrians need to be vigilant at all times, especially those with young children and on black-and-white pedestrian crossings, where it is not uncommon to see mothers with prams, and old people with walking sticks, running a gauntlet of cars. The 'green man' crossings also hold dangers because traffic can turn right or left even when the sign is illuminated.

Belgian Railways' trains often seem full of Walloons heading for the coast or one of the historic Flemish cities, while the Flemings find the Ardennes to their liking. Inter-City (IC) and Inter-Regional (IR) services are fast and comfortable. Local (L) trains, as well as being slow, seem to have been deliberately designed for discomfort. Yet travellers should have few complaints about punctuality, cleanliness and availability of seats.

Buses have a variable record. Local and urban services (often combined with trams and, in Brussels and Antwerp, the Metro) are generally very good; regional services adequate; and long-distance services either non-existent or minimal and slow. The exception is in sparsely populated areas like the Ardennes and the Kempen, which have few rail links and where buses provide the main long-distance transport.

Checking locations and directions on a tourist expedition

Visitors must get used to unfamiliar names for familiar places – Brugge instead of Bruges, for example

ATTITUDES AND ETIQUETTE

Belgians like to be treated as individuals and accord others similar treatment. Even in Bruges, where the locals' patience is sorely tried by living in a bursting-at-the-seams open-air museum, they accept their fate with good grace.

Encountering people poses few problems in such a densely populated country; meeting them does. Invitations to Belgians' homes are handed out with a parsimony that suggests fears for the family silver. Yet at a more basic level, in cafés and restaurants, few nations are more convivial or willing to discourse on all matters under the sun.

Belgian courtesy rarely extends to the formula 'how-are-you-this-morning-have-a nice-day' variety, and fawning is not to be expected. If anything, waiters in the stuffier establishments often appear brusque and ill-tempered, although an ironic humour may underlie this. When Belgians encounter genuine arrogance, they are quite prepared to create a scene.

LIFESTYLE

It is an exaggeration, but not much of one, to say that in Belgium lifestyle equals eating and drinking. Of all the food-and-drink-obsessed countries in the world, this one would surely lift the trophy in any competition.

To partake of the Belgian experience, visitors must spend a great deal of time seated at a table, waving cutlery over something as humble as a steak and French fries or one of many regional specialities, or quaffing an artisanal beer from its own individual glass (see pages 162–73).

Prices, however, are not exactly cheap. One way to minimise cost is, as many Belgians do, to order the *plat du jour/dagschotel* (dish of the day), which is always reasonably priced. For those on very restricted budgets, the bigger railway stations and department stores have acceptable restaurants, while the numerous snack bars, the *friterie/frituur* (French fries kiosk) and bar snacks are useful standbys.

WHAT TO SEE

'One must live in Brussels and loiter during long afternoons in the crowded, narrow, sloping streets of the lower town, lunch in the little restaurants in the neighbourhood of the Grand-Place ... and somehow learn to know and appreciate the tang and flavour of the local accent, and, by slow degrees, find one's way into and be accepted by the great heart of the city that is not like any other in the world.'

BRAND WHITLOCK,
US Ambassador to Belgium before World War I.

Bruxelles/Brussel (Brussels)

*B*russels' position, geographically and politically, neatly encapsulates the complex country of which it is capital. It sits almost exactly on the border between Dutch-speaking Flanders and French-speaking Wallonia, which on a wider scale translates into the age-old divide between Europe's Germanic north and Latin south. But in Belgium things are never quite so simple.

The city lies within Flemish Brabant province (there is also a Walloon Brabant). Brussels is, however, part of neither, being instead a region in its own right called Brussels Capital. Officially bilingual, French and Flemish, the existence of a large expatriate population helps tip the balance in the direction of French.

Brussels is not only the capital of Belgium (although a fair number of Belgians apparently wish that Belgium did not exist) – it is also the capital of Flanders, much to the annoyance of the Walloons, who have selected Namur as their capital. And it is the *de facto* capital of Europe, although a fair number of Europeans apparently wish that Europe did not exist, and much to the annoyance of other cities contending for the European crown.

Confused? Well, don't be. Brussels has an endearing habit of getting on with everyday life, leaving the perenially squabbling politicians to sort out what is largely a mess of their own making. Not much of the talk in cafés and restaurants is of such things. Perhaps the Bruxellois, aware of their long history of being caught in the middle of other people's quarrels, find today's difficulties refreshingly minor and simple by comparison.

With a population of about a million, Brussels sprawls among the low hills of Brabant. It is an agglomeration, a metropolitan area comprising 19 communes (local government districts), only one of which is actually called Brussels (Bruxelles in French; Brussel in Dutch). This is the old city centre, within the pentagonal or heart-shaped inner ring road that follows the course of the now-demolished city wall.

Vanishing river

Until the late 19th century, Brussels was a riverside city, built along the banks of the River Senne. In a decision that in retrospect seems astonishing, the City Fathers concluded that the river was unsanitary, unsightly, prone to flooding, and stood in the way of their ambitious boulevard-building programme. So they got rid of it.

Bricked over and hidden away out of sight, the Senne continues on its subterranean way, no doubt wondering what it did to deserve such a fate. Whatever Brussels may have gained in this bargain, it undoubtedly lost the riverside ambience that many other great cities take for granted.

Not that it lacks charm. Any city that can boast a historic pearl like the Grand-Place/Grote Markt, surely Europe's most perfect square, has enough to go around. And although the suppression of the Senne has been matched by enthusiastic demolition of architectural treasures in favour of office blocks, there are signs that the tide is turning towards restoration and preservation.

Through all these trials, the Bruxellois, natives and incomers alike, have got on with enjoying themselves.

After dark, outside the old centre, many streets seem entirely deserted, yet a closer look shows bars and restaurants bursting at the seams.

BRUSSELS CITY CENTRE

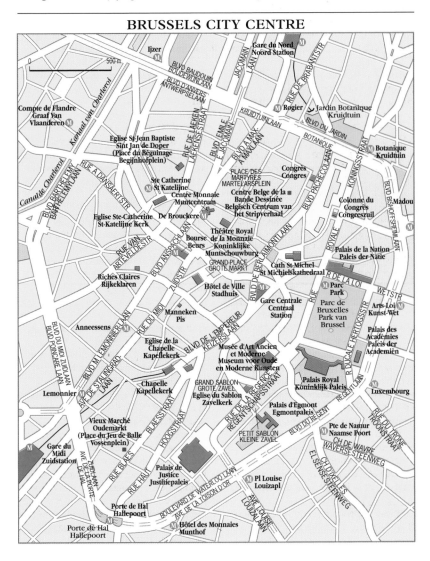

The Atomium has become a symbol of Brussels

ATOMIUM

You cannot easily miss this spectacular monument that has become a symbol of Brussels. Comprising nine giant metal spheres linked by tubular rods to represent the atomic structure of iron, the Atomium was opened in 1958 for that year's World Expo in Brussels. Inside the topmost sphere an observation deck gives a superb circular panorama of the city. Most of the interior is occupied by a 'walk-through' exhibition on human genetics.

Boulevard du Centenaire/Eeuwfeestlaan (tel: (02) 477 0977). Open: 1 April to 31 August, daily 9.30am–8pm; 1 September to 31 March, daily 9.30am–6pm. Admission charge. Metro: Heizel/Heysel.

KINEPOLIS

Said to be the world's biggest cinema complex, Kinepolis boasts 28 comfortable wide-screen theatres, and an IMAX 'wrap-around' screen, some with CD and all with the high-tech THX sound system, which should guarantee a memorable visit (always assuming the movie is good). Films are shown in their original language (usually English) with French and Dutch subtitles.

Bruparck (tel: (02) 474 2600). Open: daily 2pm, 5pm, 8pm and 10.30pm. Admission charge. Metro: Heizel/Heysel.

MINI-EUROPE

Some of the finest creations of the European spirit are on display in this miniature world, which takes the European Union as its theme. The scale is 1:25 but the effect is impressive. Among others, there are the Parthenon, the Leaning Tower of Pisa, Big Ben, the Arc de Triomphe and the Brandenburg Gate, as well as equally scaled-down engineering feats such as the Channel

BRUPARCK

A relatively new theme park in Brussels' northern suburbs, beside the Brussels Exhibition Centre and the Atomium, Bruparck Amusement Complex contains several attractions, some of which have acquired an international reputation.

It is convenient to group all the attractions under the Bruparck heading, although some, such as the Atomium, are just outside the park. The quickest way from the city centre is by Metro 1A (direction Heizel/Heysel). Once there, it is cheaper to buy a 'combination ticket' if you plan to visit more than one attraction.

Tunnel and the Ariane rocket.
_Bruparck (tel: (02) 478 0550). Open: 25
March to 30 June and 1 September to 1
November, daily 9.30am–6pm; 21 July to
20 August, daily 9.30am–midnight; 1 July
to 31 August, daily 9.30am–8pm; 2
November to 7 January, daily 10am–6pm.
Admission charge. Metro: Heizel/Heysel._

OCÉADE/OCEADIUM

An indoor aquatic paradise complete with
giant flumes, wave machine, plastic
beaches and palm trees. Océade is the
place for pretending you are on a two-
hour Caribbean holiday, especially in
winter when you can swim outside in
heated water while it snows. In summer it
also has its attraction, and children seem
to love it at any time. On weekend
evenings there is often live music in the
attached bar.
_Bruparck (tel: (02) 478 4320). Open: 1
April to 30 June, Tuesday to Thursday
2–10pm. All year: Friday 2–11pm,
Saturday 10am–11pm, Sunday
10am–10pm. Admission charge. Metro:
Heizel/Heysel._

PARC DES EXPOSITIONS/ TENTOONSTELLINGSPARK (EXHIBITIONS PARK)

Belgium's main exhibition centre, where
such prestige events as the Car Show,
Travel Fair and Ideal Homes Exhibition
are held. The giant pavilions, some from
the 1930s, show how the style of this kind
of building has evolved from 'triumphalist'
architecture to the severely practical.
_Place de Belgique/Belgiëplein (tel: (02) 477
0457). Open: daily. Admission charge.
Metro: Heizel/Heysel._

PLANETARIUM

Situated just outside the Bruparck
complex itself, the Brussels Planetarium
offers fascinating glimpses of the Belgian
sky at night.
_Avenue de Bouchout/Bouchoutlaan 10
(tel: (02) 478 9526). Open: a complex
and changeable schedule means it is best
to telephone in advance. Admission charge.
Metro: Heizel/Heysel._

THE VILLAGE

An imitation Flemish-style village. Instead
of houses, however, its buildings are
given over to a mixed bag of restaurants
and cafés, some better than others, but
which are at least convenient for
Bruparck's many attractions. There is
also a children's playground.
_Bruparck (tel: (02) 477 0377). Open:
daily. Free. Metro: Heizel/Heysel._

Mini-Europe offers a giant's perspective on the
finest European creations

Grand-Place/Grote Markt

*B*russels' historic Main Square bids fair to be considered one of the most handsome squares in Europe. Its 17th-century Flemish Renaissance-style trading and mercantile guild-houses, glittering with gold filigree, exude a calm dignity.

This has always been the heart of Brussels, although the city's turbulent history has laid it low on more than one occasion. Blood has flowed on the venerable cobbles but so too have dazzling processions honouring emperors and empresses. Jean Cocteau called it 'the richest theatre in the world'.

It is a living, working square, however, with private houses, cafés, restaurants, shops, a disco, banks and a hotel. With two exceptions its buildings are not museums. Most, but not all of them, can be visited.

LE CORNET/DEN HOREN (THE HORN)

This notable house of the Sailors' Guild has a gable that suggests the stern of a 17th-century sailing ship.
Grand-Place/Grote Markt 6.

LE CYGNE/DE ZWANE (THE SWAN)

Formerly the Butchers' Guild House, the Swan is now an up-market

restaurant, Le Cygne.
Grand-Place/Grote Markt 9.

HÔTEL DE VILLE/STADHUIS (TOWN HALL)

The late Gothic-style Town Hall dates from the 15th century. Its façade's vast array of sculptures includes some visual jokes, such as St Michael slaying a Devil who has woman's breasts.

Brussels city council meets here, in a mahogany-lined room surrounded by mirrors, and holds conferences in a chamber adorned with tapestries.
Grand-Place/Grote Market (southwest side) (tel: (02) 512 7554). Open (for guided tours only): Tuesday 11.30am and 3.15pm, Wednesday 3.15pm, Sunday 12.15pm, closed Monday and Thursday to Saturday. Admission charge.

MAISON DES BRASSEURS (BREWERS' GUILD-HOUSE)

The headquarters of the brewers' trade association and their guild, the Knights of the Mash Staff. There is also a museum of brewing. Belgium produces

The soaring spire of the Town Hall, a notable landmark in the Grand-Place

A popular and colourful feature of the Grand-Place is the daily flower market

more than 400 kinds of beer and the nominal entrance fee includes a taste of the finished product.
Grand-Place/Grote Markt 10 (tel: (02) 511 4987). Open: daily 10am–5pm. Admission charge.

MAISON DU ROI/KONINGSHUIS (KING'S HOUSE)

Dating from 1887, this impressive neo-Gothic building houses the Musée de la Ville de Bruxelles/Stedelijk Museum van Brussel (Brussels Municipal Museum). There are also the 500 or so costumes of Manneken-Pis (see page 37).
Grand-Place/Grote Markt. (tel: (02) 511 2742). Open: 1 April to 30 September, Monday to Thursday 10am–12.30pm, 1.30–5pm, Saturday and Sunday 10am–1pm, closed Friday; 1 October to 31 March, Monday to Thursday 10am–1pm, 1.30–4pm, Saturday and Sunday 10am–1pm; closed Friday. Admission charge.

MAISON DES TAILLEURS/ KLEERMAKERSHUIS (TAILORS' HOUSE)

The house is topped by a statue of Saint Boniface, who is missing a vital item of underwear!
Grand-Place/Grote Markt 24–5.

LE PIGEON/DE DUIF (THE PIGEON)

Victor Hugo lived here during 1851, above what is now a shop selling lace.
Grand-Place/Grote Markt 26–7.

TOURIST INFORMATION

Tourist Information Brussels (TIB) is located in the Town Hall, Grand-Place (tel: (02) 513 8940). Open: Monday to Saturday, 9am–6pm; Sunday, 9am–6pm summer and 10am–2pm winter. Closed Sunday, between 1 December and 28 February.

The Abbey of La Cambre, an atmospheric location near busy Avenue Louise/Louizalaan

GREEN BRUSSELS

For a city of one million people, Brussels has an astonishing number, extent and variety of parks. These range from islands of tranquillity in the centre to an ancient forest that stretches far beyond the suburbs. The following are some of the more interesting or strategically located.

ABBAYE DE LA CAMBRE/TER KAMERENABDIJ (ABBEY OF LA CAMBRE)

An old Cistercian abbey, now occupied by an art school and a geographic institute. Surrounded by gardens with pools and fountains, the abbey and neighbouring 13th-century church of Notre-Dame de la Cambre/Onze-Lieve-Vrouw-Terkameren form an atmospheric retreat in a busy neighbourhood.
Ixelles/Elsene. Avenue Louise/Louizalaan.

BOIS DE LA CAMBRE/TER KAMERENBOS (LA CAMBRE WOOD)

Brussels' biggest and most popular park is the city's lung, a place to sunbathe and play on the grass in good weather and take bracing walks at other times. At its heart is a pond with a little island called Robinson's Island, reached by a two-minute journey on an electrically operated pontoon.
Begins at the southern end of Avenue Louise/Louizalaan.

ETANGS D'IXELLES/VIJVERS VAN ELSENE (IXELLES PONDS)

There used to be a string of ponds in the little valley of the Maelbeek stream, but only two remain. These have been landscaped and, along with their gardens, make a pleasant walk in an area surrounded by town houses in art nouveau style.
Ixelles/Elsene. Avenue Général de Gaulle/Général de Gaullelaan.

FÔRET DE SOIGNES/ ZONIENWOUD (SOIGNES FOREST)

Although the forest retains only a third of its 19th-century area, at 4,400 hectares it is still a fair-sized extent of trees and undergrowth. Access is simplified by many walking, cycling and horse-riding paths that have been cut through the forest, and Brussels' citizens make this their place for a day out of the city in all weathers and in any season; autumn is especially beautiful.
The forest extends from the Bois de la Cambre/Ter Kamerenbos (see above) and is

reached by roads leaving Brussels to the southeast.

MUSÉE VICTOR HORTA/VICTOR HORTAMUSEUM (VICTOR HORTA MUSEUM)

Horta's own house, where he lived from 1901 to 1919, perfectly represents the flowing lines, natural shapes and use of light and colour that characterises art nouveau.
Ixelles/Elsene. Rue Américaine/ Amerikaansestraat 23–25 (tel: (02) 537 1692). Open: Tuesday to Sunday 2–5.30pm, closed Monday. Admission charge.

PARC DE BRUXELLES/PARK VAN BRUSSEL (BRUSSELS' PARK)

See the Royal Road section (pages 44–5).

PARC JOSAPHAT/ JOSAPHATPARK (JOSAPHAT PARK)

A surprisingly 'natural' park in a part of the city not noted for its scenic delights. Josaphat has ponds, a bird-and-animal enclosure, sculptures, a bandstand and areas of open grass as well as woodland.
Schaerbeek/Schaarbeek. Boulevard Lambermont/Lambermontlaan.

SQUARE AMBIORIX AND SQUARE MARIE-LOUISE/MARIA-LOUIZA

A small connected double park with grottoes, miniature lake and fountains. Many of the Euro-civil servants from the nearby European Commission offices use the parks for lunchtime strolls. An added attraction is the surrounding art nouveau-style residential district.
Between Chaussée de Louvain/ Leuvensesteenweg and Rue de La Loi/Wetstraat. Metro: Schuman.

Brussels is renowned for its wealth of art nouveau architecture

ART NOUVEAU

Brussels has been called the 'capital of art nouveau', having been blessed with the finest architecture of this turn-of-the-century style. Property 'developers' and local government ignorance have conspired to destroy some buildings, but many remain to dazzle the eye.

Foremost proponent of art nouveau was Brussels architect Victor Horta, whose students continued the tradition. The Solvay Mansion, the cafés De Ultieme Hallucinatie and Falstaff (see page 171), the Waucquez Warehouse, which houses the Belgian Comic Strip Centre (see page 38), the Tassel House, the florist De Backer, Square Ambiorix and Square Marie-Louise/Maria-Louiza offer superb examples of the genre.

CAPITAL OF EUROPE

There is, officially, no such thing as a capital of Europe, but Europeans talk about Brussels in much the same way as Americans talk about Washington. This is not only because the European Parliament is there (Strasbourg and Luxembourg share that distinction) but because it is home to the European Commission, the 'Eurocrats' who often appear to be the driving force behind the European ideal.

Brussels can look forward to a future as one of the world's centres of political power, yet the urge to flow with the European tide has not been cost free. The city is changing too fast and in the wrong direction for some residents. Stresses and strains are beginning to show.

Locked in the ivory tower of its

Symbols of Europe in buildings, people, flags and costumes

headquarters, the European Commission is variously seen as a group of power-hungry manipulators, greedy mandarins with first-class tickets on the Euro gravy train, or as Europe's last best hope for overcoming the divisions that have caused so much grief in the past.

The Eurocrats' influence on Brussels bears no relation to their number (there are some 7,000 of them). High salaries, low taxes, long holidays, big cars, padded expense accounts and easy hours are reckoned

to be a Eurocrat's lot.

Their presence has spawned a cosmopolitan Euro-neighbourhood of cafés, restaurants and pubs. There are even shops selling all manner of souvenirs stamped with the European symbol: a circle of 12 gold stars on a blue background. Nearby Square Ambiorix and Square Marie-Louise enclose an ornamental park with a fountain, pool and grottoes, where the civil servants take their ease. It seems hardly surprising that the 'Ode To Joy' from Beethoven's Ninth Symphony has been chosen as the European anthem.

Strolling in the Saint Hubert Royal Galleries

HISTORIC CENTRE

The area around the Grand-Place/Grote Markt (see pages 30–1) has many of the places that make Brussels an often surprising city, its lack of a distinctive character more than compensated for by a wealth of historical interest.

BOURSE/BEURS (STOCK EXCHANGE)

An ornate and solid-looking Second Empire-style building dating from 1873, this was formerly Brussels' temple to the gods of capitalism.

Rue Henri Maus/Henri Mausstraat 2 (tel: (02) 509 1211). Open: guided tours on request, Monday to Friday. Admission free. Metro: Bourse/Beurs.

CATHEDRALE SAINT-MICHEL/ SINT-MICHIELS KATHEDRAAL (SAINT MICHAEL'S CATHEDRAL)

Although only designated a cathedral in 1961, this magnificently ethereal Gothic extravaganza was begun in 1226 and stands comparison with Europe's finest cathedrals. The 16th-century Habsburg Emperor Charles V took a personal interest in its decoration, donating the superb stained-glass windows.

Place Sainte-Gudule/Sint-Goedeleplein (tel: (02) 217 8345). Open: summer, 7am to 7pm; winter 7am to 6pm. Admission free. Central Station.

EGLISE SAINT-NICOLAS/SINT-NIKLAASKERK (CHURCH OF SAINT NICHOLAS)

An island of peace, the 11th-century Romanesque church was overlaid with Gothic style in the 14th. Rebuilt several times (notably after the French bombardment of Brussels in 1695) it still shows traces of its original rough construction, and displays paintings, gold reliquaries and the Vladimir Icon, a Madonna and Child by a Greek artist at Constantinople in 1131.

Rue-au-Beurre/Boterstraat 1 (tel: (02) 513 8022). Open: daily. Admission free. Adjacent to the Stock Exchange.

GALERIES ROYALES SAINT-HUBERT/KONINKLIJKE SINT-HUBERTUS GALERIJEN (SAINT HUBERT ROYAL GALLERIES)

Said to be Europe's first shopping mall, built between 1846 and 1847 (see pages 47 and 138).

Access from Rue du Marché-aux-Herbes/Grasmarkt and Rue de l' Ecuyer/Schildknaapstraat. Open: permanently, but shops only during normal hours.

HOTEL RAVENSTEIN

Not a hotel, but a 15th-century palace. Now partly demolished, its remnant is divided between a restaurant and the headquarters of an engineering federation, but the gabled, red-brick towers and arches and a tranquil courtyard give some idea of the character of Burgundian-era Brussels. *Rue Ravenstein/Ravensteinstraat 1–3. Not open to the public (except the restaurant), but the courtyard may be visited. Behind Central Station.*

MANNEKEN-PIS

The Brussels civic authorities have (not without qualms) accepted the tourists' verdict and welcomed this fountain of a little boy, swaggeringly doing what comes naturally, as a symbol of the city. The diminutive statue dates from 1619 (although a replica occupies the site, the original being prone to theft and damage).

Many legends exist to explain his piddling activity – one is that he saved the Town Hall by extinguishing a sputtering bomb, using the first thing that came to hand. Occasionally, he can be seen wearing one of 500 or so ceremonial costumes, which are displayed at the Brussels Municipal Museum (see page 31). *Corner of Rue du Chêne/Eikstraat and Rue de l'Etuve/Stoofstraat.*

PLACE DES MARTYRS/ MARTELARSPLEIN (MARTYRS' SQUARE)

An 18th-century square that was later dedicated to Brussels patriots killed during Belgium's 1830 struggle for independence from the Netherlands. An underground crypt contains the martyrs' remains. *Connected to the Rue Neuve/Nieuwestraat by the Rue Saint-Michel/Sint-Michielsstraat.*

PLACE DU GRAND-SABLON/ GROTE ZAVELPLEIN (MAIN SABLON SQUARE)

The bigger of two adjacent squares (see Place du Petit-Sablon/Kleine Zavelplein below), renowned for its chic reputation. Antiques are big business here and there is a highly regarded weekend antiques market (see page 144) in front of Notre-Dame du Sablon/Onze-Lieve-Vrouw-op-Zavel (Our Lady of the Sablon Church). A distinctive old part of the city, its patrician homes now house boutiques, galleries and cafés. *The square is separated from its smaller neighbour by Rue de la Régence/Regentschapsstraat.*

PLACE DU PETIT-SABLON/ KLEINE ZAVELPLEIN (LITTLE SABLON SQUARE)

The Little Sablon is an island of tranquillity in the city centre. While it also has antiques shops and restaurants, its main virtue lies in the small ornamental garden with fountain and pool, surrounded by 48 columns holding bronze figures representing Brussels' medieval guilds. *The square is separated from its bigger neighbour by Rue de la Régence/Regentschapsstraat.*

Weekend antiques market held in the main Sablon Square

THEATRE ROYAL DE LA MONNAIE/KONINKLIJKE MUNTSCHOUWBURG (ROYAL MINT THEATRE)

Belgium's revolution against Dutch domination erupted at this neo-classical opera and ballet theatre (see page 150) in 1830 when, during a performance of the opera *La Muette de Portici*, a singer sang a patriotic aria which was instantly translated into action on the streets.

Place de la Monnaie/Muntplein (tel: (02) 218 1211). Open: guided tours on request.

MUSEUMS

There are over 60 museums in Brussels. As with other important places, many of the finest are concentrated in the centre, but enough are in outlying areas to add interest to a visit to these districts.

AUTOWORLD

One of the world's top collections of vintage and classic cars, including rare Belgian models such as the Minerva and Imperia marques. Also showing the development of the motor-car from 1896. *Parc du Cinquantenaire/Jubelpark (tel: (02) 736 4165). Open: 1 April to 30 September, daily 10am–6pm; 1 October to 31 March, daily 10am–5pm. Admission charge. Metro: Mérode.*

CENTRE BELGE DE LA BANDE DESSINEE/BELGISCH CENTRUM VAN HET STRIPVERHAAL (BELGIAN COMIC STRIP CENTRE)

Houses collections of famed comic strip series, including Lucky Luke, Thorgal and Asterix. Pride of place, however, goes to Tintin, the youthful sleuth whose globe-trotting adventures were the brainchild of the late 'Hergé', Belgian cartoonist Georges Remi. *Rue des Sables/Zandstraat 20 (tel: (02) 219 1980). Open: Tuesday to Sunday 10am–6pm, closed Monday. Admission charge. Off Boulevard de Berlaymont/Berlaymontlaan.*

INSTITUT ROYAL DES SCIENCES NATURELLES/KONINKLIJKE INSTITUUT VAN NATUURWETENSCHAPPEN (ROYAL INSTITUTE OF NATURAL SCIENCE)

A hands-on, interactive museum, having been totally renovated and modernised for its 150th anniversary in 1996. The natural world is on display here, from prehistoric to modern times. There are dinosaur skeletons, a marine tank, ecology displays and dioramas. Star

Ferraris take the limelight outside Autoworld

attraction must be the animated dinosaurs from Dinamation.

Chaussée de Wavre/Waversesteenweg 260 (tel: (02) 627 4238). Open: Tuesday to Saturday 9.30am–4.45pm, Sunday 9.30am–6pm, closed Monday. Admission charge. Quartier Léopold Railway Station.

MUSÉE DE LA GUEUZE/ MUSEUM VAN DE GUEUZE (GUEUZE MUSEUM)

A 'living museum' founded in 1900 specialising in the tradition of making Brussels' beers, many of them fruit-based, or fermented without yeast, like *gueuze*, *kriek* and *faro* (see pages 172–3).

Rue Gheude/Gheudestraat 56 (tel: (02) 520 2891). Open: Monday to Friday 8.30am– 4.30pm. 1 January to 30 May and 15 October to 31 December, Saturday 10am–5pm; 1 June to 14 October, 10am–1pm. Admission charge. Metro: Lemmonier.

Tintin's moon rocket at the Belgian Comic Strip Centre

FAMOUS BELGIANS

As well as important artists, such as Van Eyck, Brueghel, Rubens and Van Dyck (see pages 70–1), several other, more modern Belgians have had an impact on the world's consciousness.

These include Leo Baekeland (1863–1944), a Belgian-born chemist who invented Bakelite, the first plastic; Jacques Brel (1929–78), whose poetic songs and emotional delivery left an indelible mark on popular music; César Franck (1822–90), composer and musician, particularly noted for organ works; Hergé (1907–83), real name Georges Remi, a cartoonist who produced the Tintin series; Victor Horta (1861–1947), art nouveau architect who virtually invented the genre (see page 33); René Magritte (1898–1967), surrealist painter whose art played subtle tricks with 'reality'; Hercules Poirot, one of the great fictional detectives, the flighty, pernickety Belgian of Agatha Christie's imagination became a Hollywood star in films like *Death on the Nile*; Adolphe Sax (1814–94), inventor of the saxophone; Georges Simenon (1903–90), the novelist best known for his Maigret books (see page 109).

MUSÉE DU COSTUME ET DE LA DENTELLE/MUSEUM VOOR HET KOSTUUM EN DE KANT (COSTUME AND LACE MUSEUM)

Illustrates the importance the textile (and particularly lace) industry had for Brussels. Contains many superb displays of costumes and other examples of silk wares, dating from the 17th century onwards.

Rue de la Violette/Violetstraat 6 (tel: (02) 512 7709). Open: daily 10am–12.30pm, 1.30–5pm. Admission charge.

MUSÉE DU FOLKLORE/MUSEUM VOOR VOLKSKUNDE (BRUSSELS FOLKLORE MUSEUM)

Installed in an imposing 14th-century tower that is among the last vestiges of Brussels' old city wall, the museum provides a charming glimpse of the world of Belgian carnival and childhood by way of dolls and puppets.

Porte de Hal/Hallepoort (tel: (02) 534 1518). Open: Tuesday to Sunday 10am–5pm, closed Monday. Admission charge. Metro: Porte de Hal/Hallepoort.

MUSÉE ROYAL DE L'AFRIQUE CENTRALE/ KONINKLIJKE MUSEUM VAN MIDDEN AFRIKA (ROYAL MUSEUM OF CENTRAL AFRICA)

Recalls Belgium's colonial era in the Congo (now Zaïre). Set in a former royal estate, the museum is in the grandiose style favoured around 1910. Its exhibitions cover Africa as well as ethnography and environment on a global scale.

Leuvensesteenweg 13, Tervuren (tel: (02) 769 5211). Open: Tuesday to Sunday, 16 March to 15 October 9am–5.30pm; 16 October to 15 March 10am–4.30pm. Admission charge. Tervuren.

MUSÉE ROYAL DE L'ARMÉE ET DE L'HISTOIRE MILITAIRE/ KONINKLIJKE MUSEUM VAN HET LEGER EN VAN KRIJGSGESCHIEDENIS (ROYAL MUSEUM OF THE ARMY AND MILITARY HISTORY)

Displays a vast collection of weaponry and other military equipment dating from the days of the Frankish knights, through 12 centuries to the present day. The range of devices for bringing about untimely death is either fascinating or horrifying, according to one's taste. A section on armoured vehicles and aircraft adds to the visual impact of the exhibits.

Parc du Cinquantenaire/Jubelpark 3 (tel: (02) 733 4493). Open: Tuesday to Sunday 9am–noon, 1–4.45pm, closed Monday. Free. Metro: Mérode.

MUSÉES ROYAUX D'ART ET D'HISTOIRE/KONINKLIJKE MUSEA VOOR KUNST EN GESCHIEDENIS (ROYAL MUSEUMS OF ART AND HISTORY)

The ancient world is the theme of this light and airy museum, which has a fine collection of exhibits from the dawn of civilisation. Among the sculptures, everyday objects and dioramas is a superb model of Imperial Rome in the era of Constantine.

Parc du Cinquantenaire/Jubelpark 10 (tel: (02) 741 7211). Open: Tuesday to Friday 9.30am–5pm, weekend 10am–5pm, closed Monday. Free. Metro: Mérode.

MUSÉES ROYAUX DES BEAUX-ARTS/KONINKLIJKE MUSEA VOOR SCHONE KUNSTEN (ROYAL FINE ARTS MUSEUMS)

The Musée d'Art Ancien/Museum van Oude Kunst (Museum of Classic Art) has paintings by Brueghel (Elder and Younger) and Rubens, as well as Van Gogh, Gauguin, Renoir, Jordaens, Ensor, Seurat, Rops and many others. The underground Musée d'Art Moderne/Museum van Moderne Kunst (Museum of Modern Art) includes Magritte, Dalí, Permeke, Dufy and Delvaux.

Rue de la Régence/Regentschapsstraat 3 and Place Royale/Koningsplein 1 (tel: (02) 508 3211/513 9630). Open: (Classic) Tuesday to Sunday 10am–noon, 1–5pm, closed Monday and public holidays; (Modern) Tuesday to Sunday

The Royal Fine Arts Museums offer a choice of classic or modern art

10am–1pm, 2–5pm, closed Monday and public holidays. Free. Adjacent to Royal Palace.

METRO ART

Brussels' Metro system is the setting for a permanent exhibition of art. Given a brief to 'amuse and astonish' the travelling public, artists have taken the drab surroundings of more than 50 stations and transformed them with works of the imagination.

Top Belgian artists, including Pierre Alechinsky, Roger Raveel and Roger Somville, have accepted commissions. Somville's _Notre Temps_ (Our Time) is at Hankar station, Paul Delvaux's _Nos Vieux Trams Bruxellois_ (Our Old Brussels Trams) at the Bourse/Beurs, Emile Dubrunfaut's tapestry _La Terre en Fleur_ (The

Flowering Earth) at Louise/Louiza. Tintin gets in the picture with a mural at Stockel/Stokkel station.

Viewing this 'gallery' could not be simpler: buy a one-day Metro-pass and go underground.

OUTSIDE THE CENTRE

ARC DU CINQUANTENAIRE/ JUBELBOOG (GOLDEN JUBILEE ARCH)

A monumental statement of national pride, in the 19th-century Golden Jubilee Park. Crowned by a four-horse chariot and flanked by colonnaded porticoes lined with mosaics, the arch symbolises the country's unity.
Parc du Cinquantenaire/Eeuwfeestpark. Metro: Mérode.

BASILIQUE NATIONALE DU SACRÉ-COEUR/NATIONALE BASILIEK VAN HET HEILIG HART (NATIONAL BASILICA OF THE SACRED HEART)

Begun in 1905 somewhat in the style of a Byzantine cathedral, with a colossal dome, the basilica was completed in 1970. Its gallery offers fine views.
Parvis de la Basilique/Basiliekvoorplein 1 (tel: (02) 425 8822). Open: 1 May to 15 October, Sunday 2–5.45pm; 1 July to 31 August, Saturday and Sunday 2–5.45pm. Admission free, but charge for gallery and terrace. Koekelberg.

EUROPEAN COMMISSION

Commonly called the Palais du Berlaymont/Berlaymontpaleis (Berlaymont Palace), or just 'the Commission', this tower was home to the European Commission and a symbol of European unity – and may be once again. It is closed for the removal of asbestos.
Rue de la Loi/Wetstraat 200. Metro: Schuman.

MAISON ERASME/ERASMUS-HUIS (ERASMUS HOUSE)

Recalls the life and times of the great humanist philosopher, Erasmus, in the Anderlecht house where he lived in 1521.
Rue du Chapitre/Kapittelstraat 31, Anderlecht (tel: (02) 521 1383). Open: 10am–noon, 2–5pm, closed Tuesday and Friday. Admission charge. Metro: Saint-Guidon/Sint-Guidon.

OTAN/NAVO (NATO)

Until recent years, the nerve-centre of Western defence against the former Soviet Union and its Warsaw Pact allies. Now the North Atlantic Treaty Organisation headquarters is the 'target' of visitors from those countries.
Boulevard Léopold III/Leopold III-laan. Visits not permitted. On the road to Brussels National Airport.

PAVILLON CHINOIS/CHINEES PAVILJOEN (CHINESE PAVILION) AND TOUR JAPONAISE/JAPANSE TOREN (JAPANESE TOWER)

Two graceful structures in the form of a Chinese temple and a Japanese pagoda. Inside is a collection of antique Chinese and Japanese porcelain.
Avenue Van Praet/Van Praetlaan 44 (tel: (02) 268 1608). Open: Tuesday to Sunday 10am–5pm. Admission free.

PLACE SAINTE-CATHERINE/ SINT-KATELIJNEPLEIN (SAINT CATHERINE'S SQUARE)

A thousand years ago, the area around this square was the heart of the city, on a group of islands in the River Senne. The river was paved over a century ago.

Marché-aux-Poissons/Vismarkt (Fish Market)

Once the harbour where fishing boats docked, and now filled in. Fine seafood shops and restaurants (see page 164).
Quai-aux-Briques/Baksteenkaai and Quai-au-Bois-à-Brûler/Brandhoutkaai.

Eglise Sainte-Catherine/Sint-Katelijne Kerk (Saint Catherine's Church)

The church looks older than its 19th-century provenance, but was designed by Joseph Poelaert, who was also responsible for the Palais de Justice/Justitiepaleis (see page 44).
Place Sainte-Catherine/Sint-Katelijneplein (tel: (02) 513 3481). Open: daily 8am–5.30pm, closed Sunday afternoon.

SERRES ROYALES/KONINKLIJKE SERRES (ROYAL GREENHOUSES)

The glass-and-wrought-iron greenhouses at the Royal Palace in Laeken are memorable structures and a sensory delight with flowers and equatorial flora.
Domaine Royal/Koninklijk Domein (tel: (02) 513 8940). Open: April and May, the exact days being announced each January. Admission free.

BRUSSELS METROPOLITAN

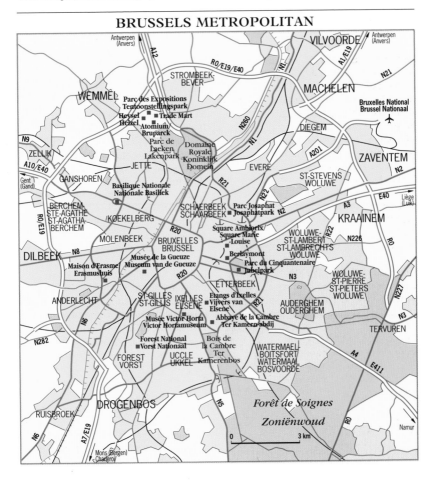

ROYAL ROAD

Many of the city's most notable buildings, including palaces, churches and museums (for museums see pages 38–41) dating from the 18th and 19th centuries, are located on the adjoining Rue Royale/Koningsstraat and Rue de la Régence/Regentschapsstraat.

PALAIS DE JUSTICE/ JUSTIEPALEIS (PALACE OF JUSTICE)

Brussels' central court is a colossal, neo-classical monument to the might and majesty of the law. Completed in 1883, the domed marble palace is entered via a great double-sided staircase flanked by statues of Cicero, Ulpian, Demosthenes and Lycurgus (symbolising Justice, Law, Mercy and Strength).

Place Poelaert (tel: (02) 508 6111). Open: Monday to Friday 9am–noon and 2–4pm. Admission free. Metro: Place Louise/Louizaplein.

The strangest things imaginable can be found at the flea market in the Marolles district

MAROLLES

Languishing in the shadow of the Justice Palace, the Marolles is Brussels' old working-class district. Poor in terms of income, but rich in community spirit, Marolliens have their own well-nigh impenetrable dialect and distinctive outlook.

Vieux Marché/Oudemarkt

Brussels' renowned flea-market takes place in the Marolles. Just about anything imaginable can be bought at this truly exotic (and cheap) market. *Place du Jeu de Balle/Vossenplein. Open: daily 7am–2pm. In the heart of the Marolles, off Rue Haute/Hoogstraat.*

PLACE ROYALE/KONINGSPLEIN (ROYAL SQUARE)

Surrounded by late 18th-century mansions, Place Royale has as its centrepiece an equestrian statue of Godefroid de Bouillon, who led the First Crusade. The graceful cobbled square is dominated by the Eglise Saint-Jacques sur-Coudenberg/Sint-Jacobskerk-op-Coudenberg (Saint James's Church on Coudenberg).

Intersection of Rue Royale/Koningsstraat and Rue de la Régence/Regentschapsstraat.

PALAIS ROYALE/KONINKLIJK PALEIS (ROYAL PALACE)

The Royal Palace seems relatively modest at first sight, with narrow ornamental front gardens. King Albert has his office here and the Belgian flag flies when he is present. The palace is also used for state receptions, although the royal family's residence is out of town, at Laeken (see page 43).

Place des Palais/Paleizenplein (tel: (02) 513 0770). Open: 21 July until a variable date in September. Admission free.

The Royal Palace in the city centre, where King Albert maintains an office

PARC DE BRUXELLES/PARK VAN BRUSSEL (BRUSSELS PARK)

This French-style landscaped park on a former royal hunting preserve is a favourite place of rest and relaxation for the district's office workers. It combines wooded trails with broad avenues that give impressive vews of the surrounding palaces.

Adjacent to Rue Royale, between the National Palace (Parliament) and the Royal Palace. Open: daily, 6am–9pm.

PALAIS DE LA NATION/PALEIS DER NATIE (NATIONAL PALACE)

The two houses of the Belgian parliament, the Senate and Chamber of Representatives, meet in this well-guarded building.

Rue de la Loi/Wetstraat 16 (tel: (02) 519 8164/515 8211). Open: Monday to Friday 10am–noon and 2–5pm, Saturday 10am–noon and 2–4pm. Closed Sundays. Admission free. Metro: Parc/Park.

COLONNE DU CONGRES/ CONGRESZUIL (CONGRESS COLUMN)

Commemorates the Independence Congress that followed Belgium's 1830 Revolution. The shaft is topped by a statue of King of the Belgians Leopold I, while the Tomb of the Unknown Soldier and the eternal flame occupy its base.

Rue Royale, midway between the National Palace and the Botanical Gardens.

JARDIN BOTANIQUE/KRUIDTUIN (BOTANIC GARDENS)

No longer used as botanic gardens, the beautiful glasshouses, dating from 1826, with their rotunda and gardens, now house a French Community Centre which hosts regular cultural events and exhibitions.

Rue Royale/Koningsstraat 236. (tel: (02) 226 1211). Open: daily 10am–6pm, plus during performances. Free, but admission charge for performances. Metro: Botanique/Kruidtuin.

Brussels City Centre Walk

This walk is through an area which contains much of the legacy that made Brussels a notable imperial and national capital. *Allow 4 hours minimum.*

Begin at Place de la Bourse/Beursplein. The route ends in the royal and monumental district (see pages 30–3, 36–7, 44–5).

1 BOURSE/BEURS (STOCK EXCHANGE)

Brussels' temple to the art of making money, the neo-classical Stock Exchange, completed in 1871, dominates a square which is surrounded by some of Brussels' most interesting cafés and restaurants (see page 171).
Cross Rue de Tabora/Taborastraat behind the Stock Exchange.

2 EGLISE SAINT-NICOLAS/SINT-NIKLAASKERK (SAINT NICHOLAS CHURCH)

A handsome little Romanesque church that seems more

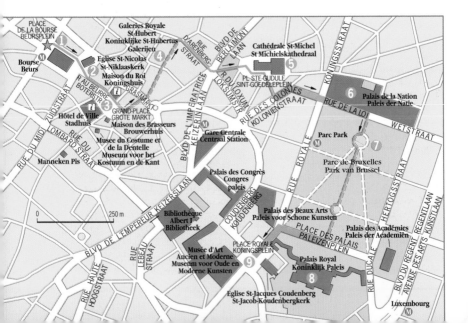

quietly spiritual than some of the city's great Gothic edifices.
Take Rue-au-Buerre/Boterstraat, past a series of lace and souvenir shops.

3 GRAND-PLACE/GROTE MARKT (MAIN SQUARE)

The magnificent Main Square is the heart of Brussels. Its Flemish Renaissance-style guild-houses, dating from the late 1690s, were once the headquarters of the medieval trading and mercantile guilds. Cafés, restaurants and shops complete the scene in what is the city's forum.
Exit the Grand-Place by Rue de la Colline/Heuvelstraat, then cross over Rue du Marché-aux-Herbes/Grasmarkt.

4 GALERIES ROYALES SAINT-HUBERT/KONINKLIJKE SINT-HUBERTUS GALERIJEN (SAINT HUBERT ROYAL GALLERIES)

Opened in 1847, Europe's first shopping mall became the model for others, such as London's Burlington Arcade. Designed in Italian neo-Renaissance style by architect Jean-Pierre Cluysenaer, the light and airy galleries feature some of Brussels' most stylish shops, cafés and restaurants.
Turn right out of the last gallery, on to Rue d'Arenberg/Arenbergstraat. Continue uphill, cross Boulevard de l'Imperatrice/Keizerinlaan to Place Sainte-Gudule/Sint-Goedeleplein.

5 CATHEDRALE SAINT-MICHEL/ SINT-MICHIELS KATHEDRAAL (SAINT MICHAEL'S CATHEDRAL)

The soaring 13th-century Gothic cathedral has an exterior of dazzlingly white stone.
Outside the Cathedral, take Rue de la

Chancellerie/Kanselarijstraat, turn left on to Rue des Colonies/Koloniënstraat and cross Rue Royale/Koningsstraat.

6 PALAIS DE LA NATION/PALEIS DER NATIE (NATIONAL PALACE)

Parliament meets here, guarded by members of all branches of the armed forces.
Cross Rue de la Loi/Wetstraat.

7 PARC DE BRUXELLES/PARK VAN BRUSSEL (BRUSSELS PARK)

Once a royal hunting ground, this handsome park's broad avenues have been designed to give monumental vistas of the city.
Exit the park on Place des Palais/Paleizenplein.

8 PALAIS ROYAL/KONINKLIJK PALEIS (ROYAL PALACE)

Although the Royal Family do not actually live in the Royal Palace, King Albert has his office here and this is where state receptions are held (see pages 16–17).
Turn left from the palace and left again to take the remaining short southern stretch of Rue Royale/Koningsstraat.

9 PLACE ROYALE/ KONINGSPLEIN

The symmetrically laid-out 'Royal' square is surrounded by 18th-century palazzo-style mansions and the neo-classical Eglise Saint-Jacques-sur-Coudenberg/Sint Jacobskerk-op-Coudenberg (Saint James's Church on Coudenberg). In the middle stands an equestrian statue of Godefroid de Bouillon, the leader of the First Crusade who died in the Holy Land in 1100.

Excursions

BRABANT

Brabant encapsulates the arrangements Belgium has made to promote harmony between Flemings and Walloons. There is a Flemish Brabant and a Walloon Brabant, while Brussels, which lies at its centre, is a virtually autonomous Belgian region.

KASTEEL VAN BEERSEL (BEERSEL CASTLE)

A magnificent 14th-century moated castle near the provincial park and recreation area at Huizingen.
Lotstraat, Beersel (tel: (02) 331 0024). Open: 1 March to 15 November, Tuesday to Sunday 10am–noon, 2–6pm, closed Monday; 16 November to 28 February, weekends only 10am–noon and 2–6pm. Admission charge. Exit 14 from Brussels Ring southwest.

Genval Lake is a pleasant and popular place for relaxing in the evening and at weekends

GENVAL

A popular place for weekend walks, Genval is a village with attractive villas, cafés and restaurants around a pretty lake with a high fountain.

Lac de Genval (Genval Lake)

The lake, created in 1904, is an idyllic spot surrounded by villas, some of which are modelled on famous buildings. For example, the Rendezvous d'Amour Pavilion, with a lighthouse-tower overlooking the lake, is based on an original at Versailles, while the Guillaume Tell Villa is based on a Swiss building associated with William Tell.
Located 0.5km from Genval railway station.

Musée de l'Eau et de la Fontaine (Water and Fountain Museum)

Houses an interesting collection of fountains as well as old water-pumps, filters and other hydraulic equipment,

plus displays on water pollution and resources.
Avenue Hoover 63 (tel: (02) 654 1923). Open: weekends and public holidays 10am–6pm. Admission charge. Adjacent to the lake.

LOUVAIN-LA-NEUVE

The Université Catholique de Louvain (Catholic University of Louvain) was located here in 1970 after a schism at Leuven University (see page 50) showed that even centuries-old centres of learning were not immune to the pressures of Belgium's French–Dutch language divide. Academic buildings, student residences, shopping and recreational areas are combined in a model garden-city, where cutting-edge ideas in architecture and town planning hold sway.
Exit 9 from the E411 southeast of Brussels (25km).

NATIONALE PLANTENTUIN (NATIONAL BOTANIC GARDENS)

The gardens form a huge estate with a moated 13th-century castle, a lake and displays that range from ornamental to tangled trees and bushes. Even when the greenhouses of the Plantenpaleis (Plant Palace) are closed, the estate's public areas are fascinating and worth visiting in their own right in any season.
Domein Van Bouchout, Brusselsesteenweg 28, Meise (tel: (02) 269 3905). Open: estate – summer: daily 9am–5.30pm, winter: daily 9am–5pm; greenhouses – from Easter to last Sunday in October, Monday to Thursday 1–4pm, Sunday and public holidays 2–5.30pm. Estate free; admission charge for greenhouses. A12 Brussels–Antwerp road, exit Meise (12km north of Brussels).

Students live and study amidst the latest architecture at Louvain-la-Neuve

PARK HOFSTADE-STRAND (HOFSTADE BEACH-PARK)

Belgians like their seaside so much they've re-created a piece of it near Mechelen, at Hofstade, where a nature reserve shares open space with a recreational lake and an artificial beach bordered by cafés and changing rooms.
Rijksdomein Hofstade (tel: (015) 611301). Open: all year. Admission free, but beach and parking charge in tourist season. Exit 11 from the E19.

VILLERS-LA-VILLE

The ruined 12th-century Cistercian abbey at Villers-la-Ville is one of Belgium's most important historic sites, and dramatically atmospheric.
Rue de l'Abbaye 53 (tel: 071 879555). Open: 1 April to 31 October, 10am–6pm (Monday and Tuesday noon–4pm); 1 November to 31 March, Wednesday, Thursday and Friday 1–5pm, weekends 11am–5pm. Admission charge. N275, 2km north of Villers-la-Ville.

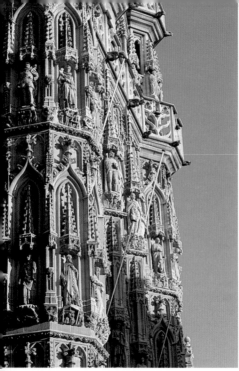

The fantastic Gothic tracery and sculptures of Leuven Town Hall

LEUVEN (LOUVAIN)

Located 15km east of Brussels, Leuven is perhaps Belgium's most surprising small city. The Katholieke Universiteit van Leuven (Catholic University of Leuven), founded in 1425, is one of Europe's oldest universities.

GROOT BEGIJNHOF (LARGE BEGUINAGE)

The 13th-century beguinage is now a residence for students from the University. The small, red-brick houses around a courtyard make an appropriately tranquil location for contemplation and study – except that Leuven's students are exponents of the 'all work and no play makes Jan a dull boy' theory of education.
Schapenstraat. As people live here, visits are restricted to a stroll around the grounds. Located off Naamsestraat, beside the River Dijle.

OUDE MARKT (OLD MARKET)

Leuven's liveliest square and centre of the town's student night-life, Oude Markt is packed with bars, restaurants and snack bars. The cobbled square was once a more sober place, its merchants' houses the town's richest quarter.
Located 100m from the Town Hall, off Naamsestraat.

STADHUIS (TOWN HALL)

Arguably Belgium's most handsome civic building, Leuven's 15th-century Town Hall in the Grote Markt (Main Square) is a flamboyant late-Gothic tracery of spires, lavishly carved façades and almost 300 statue-filled niches.
Grote Markt (tel: 016 211539). Open: Monday to Friday 11am and 3pm; weekends and public holidays 3pm only. Admission charge.

RIVER DIJLE

A fine short excursion from Leuven is along the scenic valley of the River Dijle, through Heverlee, 't Zoet Water, Sint-Joris-Weert and Sint-Agatha-Rode. This is an area of small lakes, *kastelen* (castles), pretty villages and rolling farmland.

MECHELEN (MALINES)

As well as being the seat of Belgium's Roman Catholic primate, Mechelen is a centre of tapestry, lace and carillons.

HORLOGERIE MUSEUM (CLOCK MUSEUM)

A small museum devoted to the ancient art of timekeeping, and which doubles as a workshop for making and repairing

timepieces. Exhibits include traditional grandfather clocks and curios such as 'painting clocks' – canvasses with a clock inset.
Lange Schipstraat 13 (tel: (015) 211894). Open: Monday to Saturday 10am–noon, 2–6pm, closed Sunday. Admission charge.

KONINKLIJKE MANUFACTUUR VAN WANDTAPIJTEN (ROYAL TAPESTRY MANUFACTURERS)

Belgium's last tapestry-maker (see pages 118–19) produces modern tapestries and restores old ones in a 15th-century abbey building. The company's own collection gives an insight into the art form that once dazzled Europe.
Schoutestraat 7 (tel: (015) 202905). Open: guided tour only, Saturday 10.30am. Admission free.

MUSEUM HOF VAN BUSLEYDEN (BUSLEYDEN MUSEUM)

Dating from 1503, this former stately home has been transformed into Mechelen's city museum, and has a wealth of paintings, tapestries, sculptures and furnishings. Across the courtyard is the Beiaardmuseum (Carillon Museum), featuring bells, keyboards and other mechanisms of the bell-players' art.
Merodestraat 65 (tel: (015) 202004). Open: Tuesday to Friday 10am–noon, 2–5pm, Saturday and Sunday 2–6pm, closed Monday. Admission charge. Located 200m north of the Grote Markt.

STADHUIS (TOWN HALL)

The 14th-century Lakenhalle (Cloth Hall) and its 16th-century neighbour, the Paleis van de Grote Raad (Palace of the Grand Council), form an elegant

Stepping into the 13th century inside Mechelen's Saint Rombold's Cathedral

complex in the old Main Square.
Grote Markt (tel: (015) 297655). Open: guided tours only, weekends 2pm. Admission charge.

SINT-ROMBOUTSKATHEDRAAL (SAINT ROMBOLD'S CATHEDRAL)

A sumptuous 13th-century cathedral, with a 97m-high belfry that dominates the town. Among its artworks is the *Christ on the Cross Between Two Criminals* by Van Dyck.
Grote Markt (tel: 015 201934). Open: summer – daily 10am–noon, 2–6pm; winter – daily 10am–noon, 2–5pm. Admission free.

CARILLONS

Mechelen is the centre of Belgium's carillon tradition, and the belfry of Saint Rombold's contains two 49-bell carillons and a seven-bell unit, together weighing more than 80 tonnes. There is also the Koninklijke Beiaardschool (Royal Carillon School) on the corner of Merodestraat 63 and Sint-Jansstraat (guided tours only; information from (015) 204792).

NAPOLEON'S LAST BATTLE

When the French Emperor Napoleon Bonaparte awoke on 18 June, 1815, and looked up at the Allied army occupying a low ridge near Waterloo, blocking his path, he foresaw little difficulty in brushing it aside. 'If you obey my orders well,' he told his generals, 'we shall sleep tonight in Brussels.'

The Duke of Wellington, commanding an army of British, Belgians and Dutch, hoped his 72,000 mostly raw troops could hold off Napoleon's 75,000 veterans long enough for Marshal Blücher to come up with 60,000 Prussians and take the French in the flank.

French artillery opened the battle, followed by an infantry assault on the fortified farm of Hougoumont. More French infantry advanced up the ridge, where they were greeted by heavy volleys of musketry. A British cavalry force decimated the wavering foot soldiers, then galloped on to the French artillery where they in turn were slaughtered.

The French cavalry under Marshal Ney, the 'bravest of the brave', took up the challenge, charging time after time up the slope, over a carpet of dead and wounded men and writhing horses, but fared no better against Allied infantry squares. More French infantry captured the fortified farm of La Haie-Sainte, opening the way for an attack on the Allied centre.

With the Prussians threatening his flank and rear, Napoleon gambled his future on a last roll of the dice. He threw his élite Old Guard forward at the battle's climax in a desperate effort to break Wellington's exhausted and bleeding line.

The Iron Duke's forces held fast, but only just, and the remnant of the Old Guard finally retreated under a storm of musketry, cannon balls and grapeshot. For the French, defeat turned into rout, with Napoleon himself barely escaping. But, said Wellington, 'It was the nearest run thing you ever saw in your life.'

Re-enactments and the tactical picture illustrate Waterloo's day of glory

WATERLOO

The Battle of Waterloo was not actually fought at Waterloo but a few kilometres to the south, between the hamlets of Mont-Saint-Jean and Plancenoit.

Today, the battlefield remains much as it was on 18 June 1815, when 200,000 colourfully uniformed soldiers engaged in mutual slaughter on its gently sloping farmland.

The Lion Mound – a memorial to Holland's wounded Prince William of Orange

BUTTE DU LION (LION MOUND)

Raised in 1826 by the Dutch to mark the spot where Prince William of Orange was wounded, the 40m-high conical mound is the most striking monument on the battlefield. It is capped by a cast-iron lion on a plinth and there is a fine view of the theatre of war from its summit, reached by 226 steps.
Route du Lion 252–4 (tel: (02) 385 1912). Open: 1 April to 30 September, daily 9.30am–6.30pm; October, daily 9.30am–5.30pm; 1 November to 28 February, daily 10am–4pm; March, daily 10.30am–5pm. Admission charge. Entrance through Visitor's Centre beside bus-stop.

CENTRE DU VISITEUR (VISITOR'S CENTRE)

An audio-visual presentation of the tactical picture plus an extract from the epic movie *Waterloo* give an idea of the battle's impressive scale.
Route du Lion 252–4 (tel: (02) 385 1912). Open: same opening times as Butte du Lion (Lion Mound) above. Admission charge.

HOUGOUMONT

A fortified farm which still bears the scars of battle. Plaques on the walls commemorate its heroic defence against overwhelming odds by a handful of British infantry.
Braine-l'Alleud. Hougoumont is private property, but its owners allow visits to the farmyard.

LA HAIE-SAINTE

A fortified farm that played a crucial role in the battle by shielding the centre of Wellington's line from direct assault. The French finally took the farm but with such a loss of lives and time that they were unable to exploit their success.

Chaussée de Charleroi/Bruxelles. Near the junction with Route du Lion. La Haie-Sainte can only be viewed from the outside.

MUSÉE DE CIRE (WAXWORKS MUSEUM)

Napoleon, Wellington, Blücher and other members of both sides' high command appear here in wax images.
Route du Lion 315 (tel: (02) 384 6740). Open: 1 April to 31 October, daily 9am–6.30pm; 1 November to 31 March, weekends only 10am–4.45pm. Admission charge. Opposite the Visitor's Centre.

MUSÉE DU CAILLOU (CAILLOU MUSEUM)

The Caillou farm was Napoleon's headquarters and the place where he slept before the battle. It contains many items found on the battlefield but its most fascinating exhibits are those associated with the Emperor: his campaign bed, drinking cup, map table and a bust of Napoleon by Chaudet.
Chaussée de Bruxelles 66, Vieux-Genappe (tel: (02) 384 2424). Open: 1 April to 31 October, Tuesday to Sunday 10am–6.30pm; 1 November to 31 December and 1 February to 31 March, 1.30–5pm; closed Mondays and throughout January. Admission charge. N5, after the junction with the Plancenoit road.

MUSÉE WELLINGTON (WELLINGTON MUSEUM)

Located in an old Brabant coaching inn that was used as the Duke of Wellington's headquarters, and was where he wrote the victory dispatch.
Chaussée de Bruxelles 147, Waterloo (tel: (02) 354 7806). Open: 1 April to 31 October, daily 9.30am–6.30pm; 1 November to 31 March, daily 10am–5pm. Admission charge. Waterloo village.

Napoleon's legend is alive and well at the Caillou Museum

PANORAMA DE LA BATAILLE (PANORAMA OF THE BATTLE)

The cylindrical building contains a spectacular painted diorama of a crucial phase of the battle – the massed French cavalry charge led by Marshal Ney, 'the bravest of the brave'.
Chemin des Vertes Bornes 90, Mont-Saint-Jean (tel: (02) 384 3139). Open: 1 April to 30 September, daily 9.30am–6.30pm; 1 November to 28 February, daily 10am–4pm; March daily 10.30am–5pm. Admission charge. Beside the Visitor's Centre.

THOMAS COOK'S BELGIUM

The first Thomas Cook trip to Europe in 1855 visited the battlefield of Waterloo. Although Cook later criticised the celebration of military victories in his Excursionist Magazine, *he continued to provide travel services to Waterloo.*

Vlaanderen (Flanders)

*O*ccupying the northern half of Belgium and, with some 5.5 million people, containing more than half of Belgium's population, Flanders takes in all of the Belgian coast as well as the historic cities of Antwerpen (Antwerp), Brugge (Bruges) and Gent (Ghent).

Despite having such stellar cities to choose from, Flanders has made the seemingly odd decision to select Brussels as the regional seat of government partly to retain a hold on the bilingual Euro-city that the Flemings fear may be slipping away from them. It can hardly be denied, however, that the heartland of Flemish culture lies in one of these other cities, and Ghent is usually credited with the title, though not without some dissent from its rivals.

Flanders shared Wallonia's historic role as a parade ground and battlefield for other European countries' armies, although in Flanders' case the seat of empire was often installed in one of its cities, Brussels among them.

Distinctive features

The region has a more restrained topograhy than that of the flamboyant Ardennes, even allowing for the low hills around Ronse and Geraardsbergen that have been labelled the Vlaamse Ardennen (Flemish Ardennes). The coastline and the related dunes and

FLANDERS

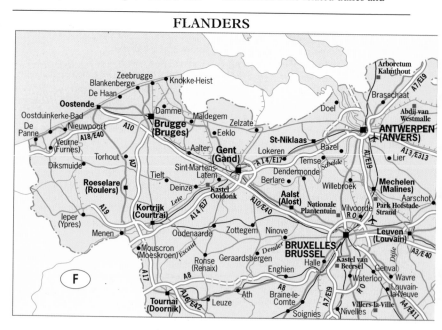

polders are its most distinctive features, along with the moors of the Kempen on the border with the Netherlands.

Visitors come to Flanders, however, for those magnificent cities, and while in doing so they may miss out on other places of interest, the decision is understandable. Each ranks as a great centre of medieval or Renaissance culture, or both. They may have arrived on the scene later, and departed earlier – partly due to the hammer blows of war – than Florence or Venice, but the comparison is far from unjust.

A group of Flemish artists from this period have had their work handed down to us under the unflattering banner of the 'Flemish Primitives'. Yet the work of Jan Van Eyck, whose *Adoration of the Mystic Lamb* still spellbinds visitors to Ghent's Saint

Bavo's Cathedral, can scarcely be thought of as 'primitive'. Nor can that of his fellow artists Rogier van der Weyden, Hans Memling and Petrus Christus (see pages 70–1.

The later works of Pieter Brueghel the Elder, Pieter Paul Rubens, Jacob Jordaens and Antony Van Dyck cemented the Flemish connection with the finest art of its day.

Architectural time-capsules

The Flemish cities are also well endowed with fine architecture, though each has a different aspect. Bruges is by any reckoning one of the handsomest cities on the planet. Centuries-old, almost perfectly preserved (or restored) buildings are reflected in the canals that wind through the city. If there is a complaint to make of Bruges (and it is not exactly a strenuous one) it is that the city may be too self-consciously pretty, too perfect, for its own good.

Antwerp and Ghent are refreshingly far from perfection, sharing many of the problems that beset cities the world over. But they retain an awesome legacy from the days when the adjective 'Flemish' symbolised style, wealth and power. In its modern diamond industry (worth 16 times that of more publicity-conscious Amsterdam), Antwerp may be said to continue the tradition.

Away from its trinity of historic cities, Flanders has more restrained attractions, though perhaps no less glittering in their way. The coast, connected from the French border to the Dutch by a tram service called the Kusttram (Coast Tram: see pages 84–5) is one, although Belgium has been cavalier in its treatment of what was once the most stylish stretch of sand in Europe.

ANTWERP

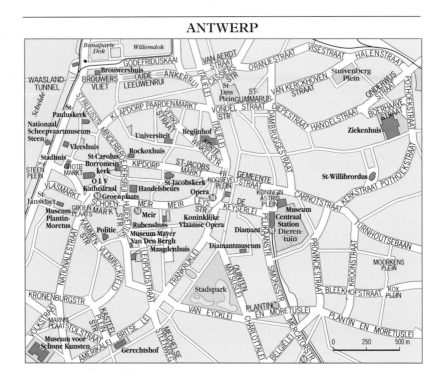

ANTWERPEN (ANTWERP)

Antwerp could be Europe's most underestimated city. Its image is little more than that of a port (Europe's second biggest), yet this is only a fraction of the story – a big fraction as a visit to dockland will show.

Having been European Capital of Culture in 1993 helped with informing the world of its associations with Rubens, Jordaens, Plantin, the Reformation, the Habsburg Empire, even the Spanish Inquisition. A hands-on visit, however, is needed to capture the city's free spirit, throbbing nightlife, animated cultural scene and memorable architecture.

BEGIJNHOF (BEGUINAGE)

One of those traditional Flemish institutions for *begijns*, religious women whose vows were somewhat less strict than those of nuns. The 16th-century Beguinage is today a restful neighbourhood of little houses and cobbled streets.
Rodestraat 39. Metro: Opera.

CENTRAAL STATION (CENTRAL STATION)

More like a soaring, marble-decorated cathedral than a railway station, Antwerp Central is a destination worth visiting in its own right.
Koningin Astridplein.

The fountain in Antwerp's Main Square depicts a legend of the city's founding

DIAMANTMUSEUM (DIAMOND MUSEUM)

In the heart of the Diamond Quarter (see box, page 61), the museum reveals the story behind the lure and lore of diamonds, from geology to high finance. It includes reproductions of famous stones and there are demonstrations of diamond-cutting and polishing.

Lange Herentalsestraat 31–3 (tel: (03) 231 8645). Open: daily 10am–5pm. Admission free. Metro: Diamant.

DIERENTUIN (ZOO)

Antwerp Zoo is renowned for its modern approach, research and conservation work with animals, particularly threatened species. It is also a marvellous family experience and its art deco architecture adds colour to this.

Koningin Astridplein 26 (tel: (03) 202 4540). Open: summer – daily 9am–6.30pm; winter – daily 9am–4.45pm. Admission charge. Central Station.

GROTE MARKT (MAIN SQUARE)

On three sides of Antwerp's beautiful Grote Markt are 16th-century Flemish *gildehuizen* (guild-houses), topped with gilded figures that glitter in the sun; on the fourth is the Renaissance Stadhuis (Town Hall). A fine fountain-sculpture depicts Silvius Brabo throwing the severed hand of the giant Antigonus into the River Scheldt.

Stadhuis, Grote Markt (tel: (03) 220 8211). Open: Monday, Tuesday, Wednesday and Friday 9am–3pm, Saturday noon–3.30pm (times subject to change due to Council business). Admission charge.

HAVEN (HARBOUR)

The harbour is a colossal industrial site (see box, page 63), covering 1,500 hectares of land, and with nearly 100km of quays and 1,000km of railway track. It is possible to tour the harbour by boat (see Boat Trips box below) and there is free access by road.

For further information, contact: Port of Antwerp, Entrepotkaai 111 (tel: (03) 205 2011).

JORDAENSHUIS (JORDAENS' HOUSE)

This was the home of Antwerp's 17th-century painter Jacob Jordaens. It is now used for exhibitions.

Reyndersstraat 6 (tel: (03) 234 3985). Open: only for special exhibitions or on request. Metro: Groenplaats.

BOAT TRIPS

The Flandria Shipping Company provides tours of the River Schelde/River Escaut (River Scheldt) and Antwerp harbour, including evening tours when the port is a fairground of lights. There are also cruises to Bruges and Oostende. NV Flandria, Haverstraat 1 (tel: (03) 231 3100). Cruises depart from the quay adjacent to the Steen (Castle).

MUSEUM VOOR HEDENDAAGSE KUNST (CONTEMPORARY ART MUSEUM)

More commonly known as MUHKA, this was once a grain warehouse, part of Antwerp's old port facilities. Behind the warehouse's original art deco façade, a collection of cutting-edge Belgian and international art is expanding to fill the enormous interior.

Leuvenstraat 16–30 (tel: (03) 238 5960). Open: Tuesday to Sunday 10am–5pm, closed Monday. Admission charge. Located 100m from riverside, south of the city centre.

MUSEUM VOOR SCHONE KUNSTEN (ROYAL FINE ARTS MUSEUM)

A neo-classical temple of art, the gallery dates from 1890 and has a powerful collection of masterpieces by the 15th-century Flemish 'Primitives', including Van Eyck, Van der Weyden and Memling. Other eras have scarcely been neglected, however, and the luminaries of the Antwerp School – Rubens, Jordaens and Van Dyck – are well represented. When these names are added to those of Brueghel the Elder, Ensor, Magritte, Permeke, Delvaux and many others, the problem is finding time to see everything.

Leopold de Waelplaats 1–9 (tel: (03) 238 7809). Open: Tuesday to Sunday 10am–5pm, closed Monday. Admission charge. Between Amerikalei and Waelstraat, south of the city centre.

ONZE-LIEVE-VROUWEKATHEDRAAL (CATHEDRAL OF OUR LADY)

The superbly light and airy cathedral, Belgium's biggest, has had its ups and downs ever since work was started on it in 1352, having been devastated by fires and the 16th-century's Iconoclastic Fury. Today, its 123m-high spire still dominates the city's skyline.

Three works by Rubens and his school embellish the interior: the lavishly baroque *Raising of the Cross,* the sombre *Descent from the Cross,* and the *Resurrection.*

Handschoenmarkt (tel: (03) 231 3033). Open: Monday to Friday 10am–5pm, Saturday 10am–3pm, Sunday and holy days 1–4pm. Admission charge. Metro: Groenplaats.

Left: café terraces surround the Cathedral of Our Lady's imposing belfry

Opposite page: the Rubens House where the Belgian master painted many of his finest works

OPENLUCHTMUSEUM VOOR BEELDHOUWKUNST MIDDELHEIM (MIDDELHEIM OPEN-AIR SCULPTURE MUSEUM)

Walking through a leafy park and gardens dotted with works of art makes a pleasant way to experience the often unusual products of modern sculpture. With works by well-known sculptors, including Auguste Rodin and Henry Moore, among many others, the park adds up to memorable experience.

Middelheimlaan (tel: (03) 828 1350). Open: Tuesday to Sunday, closed Monday: April, September, 10am–7pm; May, August, 10am–8pm; June, July, 10am–9pm; October to March, 10am–5pm. Free. Middelheim Park.

DIAMONDS

Diamonds may or may not be for ever, but they are certainly close to Antwerp's heart, as well as its wallet, bringing a sparkling $16 billion a year to the city (compared with Amsterdam's $1 billion). Antwerp is the world's centre for trade in diamonds.

Much of this activity takes place in the Diamond Quarter, a bustling but remarkably small area considering the value it generates. Alongside smoothly opulent buildings like the Hoge Raad voor Diamant (Diamond High Council) and the Beurs voor Diamanthandel (Diamond Exchange) stands a glittering parade of jewellery shops.

For further information, contact the Diamond High Council Hoveniersstraat 22 (tel: (03) 222 0511). Metro: Diamant.

PLANTIN-MORETUSMUSEUM (PLANTIN-MORETUS MUSEUM)

The French-born printer Christopher Plantin, who moved to Antwerp in 1548, established here Europe's premier printing works of the time. Among the many exhibits is a Librorium Prohibitorum, a list of 'dangerous' books banned by the Church.

Vrijdagmarkt 22 (tel: (03) 233 0294). Open: Tuesday to Sunday 10am–4.45pm, closed Monday. Admission charge. Metro: Groenplaats.

RUBENSHUIS (RUBENS HOUSE)

The great Belgian artist Pieter-Paul Rubens lived and worked in this patrician town house from 1610 until his death in 1640. The two wings of the house and its courtyard marvellously evoke the period.

Wapper 9 (tel: (03) 232 4747). Open: Tuesday to Sunday 10am–4.45pm, closed Monday. Admission charge. Metro: Meir.

Saint Charles Borromeo's Church

SINT-CAROLUS BORROMEUSKERK (SAINT CHARLES BORROMEO'S CHURCH)

Rubens was intimately involved in the design and embellishment of this early 17th-century church, employing ideas and techniques learned during his travels in Italy, which accounts in part for its sumptuous style.

Hendrik Conscienceplein 12 (tel: (03) 232 2742). Open: daily for visits except during services. Admission charge. Metro: Meir.

SINT-JACOBSKERK (SAINT JAMES'S CHURCH)

Rubens, who died in 1640, is buried in this church, whose heavily ornamented 17th-century baroque aspect overlays the cleaner Gothic lines of its 15th-century

beginnings. The artist's vault, the chief focus of interest for many, is in the Rubens Chapel, one of seven chapels that form a semicircle behind the opulent high altar. Saint James's was the favoured place of eternal rest for Antwerp's high and mighty.

Lange Nieuwstraat 73 (tel: (03) 232 1032). Open: 1 April to 31 October, Monday to Saturday 2–5pm; 1 November to 31 March, 9am–noon, closed Sunday and during services. Admission charge. Metro: Opera or Meir.

STEEN (CASTLE)

The gloomy castle dominating the Scheldt riverside in the city centre stands on the site of earlier fortifications going back to the city's foundation. The present turreted structure dates from around 1200, with a 16th-century reconstruction supplying its embellishment.

Today the Steen houses the Nationaal Scheepvaartmuseum (National Maritime Museum), which contains models of boats and exhibits on the development of shipping, while adjacent wharves have real boats and ships to explore.

Steenplein 1 (tel: (03) 232 0850). Open: Tuesday to Sunday 10am–4.45pm, closed Monday. Admission charge. Riverfront, 200m from Grote Markt.

VLAEYKENSGANG

An atmospheric old warren of cobbled courtyards, narrow passageways and higgledy-piggledy houses, which was rescued only just in time from demolition. The city-centre complex conjures up the Middle Ages, despite having been converted to apartments, restaurants, cafés and studios.

Oude Koornmarkt 16, across from the Grote Markt.

VLEESHUIS (BUTCHER'S HALL)

Despite its name and former function as a meat market and home to the Butchers' Guild, the hall is a fairy-tale structure: part turreted castle, part soaring cathedral and part patrician residence built in candy-striped layers of alternating red and white. Today it houses an applied arts museum, concentrating on Antwerp's historical contribution to this field.

Vleeshouwersstraat 38–40 (tel: (03) 233 6404). Open: Tuesday to Sunday 10am–4.45pm, closed Monday. Admission charge. Located 50m behind Jordaenskaai from the riverfront.

WIJK ZURENBORG (ZURENBORG QUARTER)

A residential neighbourhood that is a registered site, for its fascinating collection of town houses in Jugendstil, art nouveau, and a variety of other turn-of-the century styles. It seems that each architect was determined to outdo his competitors in experimentation and verve.

Cogels-Osylei and surrounding streets, adjacent to Berchem railway station.

ANTWERP HARBOUR

One of Belgium's most remarkable sights is the colossal Antwerp harbour (see page 59). Time was when sailing ships tied up at the city's doorstep to unload spices from the Orient, timber from the Baltic, and herring from the Grand Banks, but the tides of commerce have flowed away to the highly automated docks between Antwerp and the Dutch border.

Container ships, bulk-carriers, tankers; sleek greyhounds and seaworn tramps; brilliant in customised paint-jobs or fading away to rust-bucket oblivion – all are waited on by a vast retinue of machines, and some humans. Hundreds of trucks, trains and barges, each carrying its little piece of the action, hurry outwards from the hub only to be drawn in again as if by gravity.

Antwerp is one of the pumps that replenishes the world's commercial arteries. Every year, more than 16,000 ships discharge and load 100 million tonnes of cargo here, with all the port's activities contributing BF190 billion to Belgium's national income and providing 75,000 jobs.

Further information about these and the many other attractions of Antwerp is available from the Dienst voor Toerisme (Tourism Service), Grote Markt 15, B-2000 Antwerp (tel: (03) 232 0103). Open: Monday to Friday 9am–6pm, Saturday, Sunday and holidays 9am–5pm.

A representation of autumn on the wall of a house, Antwerp

Telling universal time with the Zimmer Tower's astronomical clock in Lier

AROUND ANTWERP

ABDIJ VAN WESTMALLE (WESTMALLE ABBEY)
Cistercian monks occupy the 19th-century abbey, their only concession to the world being the potent Westmalle beer which they produce.
Westmalle. Interior closed to the public, but grounds accessible. Located 2km south of Westmalle on the N12.

ARBORETUM KALMTHOUT
Near the Natuurreservaat De Kalmthoutse Heide (Kalmthout Heath Nature Reserve), an area of sand-dunes, heathland and forest beside the Dutch border, the Arboretum displays 6,000 varieties of trees, plants and shrubs.
Kalmthout (tel: (03) 666 6741). Open:

15 March to 15 November, daily 10am–5pm. Admission charge. Exit 4 from the E19.

BAZEL
A pretty country village beside the River Scheldt, noted for its 14th-century Sint-Pieterskerk (Saint Peter's Church) and castle.

Kasteel van Wissekerke (Wissekerke Castle)
A moated 16th-century castle, almost entirely rebuilt in the 19th, but not open to the public. The surrounding estate, however, has been given over to a park with duck ponds, bridges and lawns, and this can be visited.
Outside Bazel village. Free. N419, 12km from Antwerp, across the River Scheldt.

BRASSCHAAT
The Gemeentepark (Public Park) is at the centre of an area of nature reserves, woods, parks and country villas on Antwerp's doorstep. Its 19th-century, neo-classical Kasteel van Brasschaat (Brasschaat Castle) is only open to pre-arranged groups.
Gemeentepark, Brasschaat (tel: (03) 651 3300). Open: permanently. Free. Located 10km northeast of Antwerp on the N1.

DOEL
In the flat polderland across the River Scheldt from Antwerp, near the Verdronken Land van Saeftinghe (Drowned Land of Saeftinghe), Doel is a tiny fishing village protected from flooding by a dike. The dike-top offers an ideal platform for watching the busy parade of merchant ships sailing to and from Antwerp.
Close to the Dutch border, 14km northwest of Antwerp.

LIER

Lier has all the attributes of a typical small Flemish town, and a remarkable tower that enhances its character.

Zimmertoren (Zimmer Tower)

Named after Lodewijk Zimmer, a local businessman who, in 1930, set out to explain the universe to his fellow citizens. The 14th-century tower is graced with the remarkable Jubelklok (Centenary Clock), depicting the sun, moon, Zodiacal signs, seasons, tides on Lier's River Nete, and other calculations. Inside the tower, the equally fascinating Wonderklok (Wonder Clock) joins many other astronomical devices in a tribute to Zimmer's noble obsession.

Zimmerplein (tel: (03) 489 1111). Open: 1 April to 30 September, daily 9am–noon, 1–6pm; July and August, daily 9am–noon, 1–7pm; January, February, November and December, daily 9am–noon, 2–4pm; March and October, daily 9am–noon, 2–5pm. Admission charge. Located 100m from the Grote Markt.

'S-GRAVENWEZEL

The village stands in a heavily wooded area traversed by a stream called the Klein Schein, which is popular with day-trippers out for fresh air. There are traditional farms, estates and privately owned châteaux, such as the Kasteel van 's-Gravenwezel ('s-Gravenwezel Castle), in the countryside around the village.

Located 12km northeast of Antwerp on the N121.

SINT-NIKLAAS

Renowned for having Belgium's biggest Grote Markt (Main Square) – a statistic that carries weight in a country where the Grote Markt is the measure of municipal status. A flamboyant 19th-

A tranquil waterside scene in Lier

century neo-Gothic Stadhuis (Town Hall) puts the space to good use.

Located 20km southwest of Antwerp, on the N70.

TEXTIELMUSEUM VRIESELHOF (VRIESELHOF TEXTILE MUSEUM)

On a formerly private estate, close to the Albert Kanaal (Albert Canal), the museum is located in a red-brick, gabled château whose origins reach back to the 13th century. It displays lace from the 16th to 20th centuries, traditional costumes, and machines and other items from the textile trade.

Schildesteenweg 79 (tel: (03) 383 4680). Open: 1 March to 30 November, Tuesday to Friday 9am–5pm, Saturday and Sunday 10am–5pm, closed Monday. Free. Located 2km from Schilde, off the N12.

BRUGGE (BRUGES)

Because of its canals, it is not uncommon to hear Bruges described as the 'Venice of the North'. This is an unnecessary comparison, because Bruges stands on its own as a uniquely well-preserved city, ranging from medieval to modern times.

Bruges throws your sense of time out of joint, sweeping you back through the centuries. It is also an almost stagily pretty city, and if there is one criticism visitors have, it is that it seems almost too perfect.

BEGIJNHOF (BEGUINAGE)

Begijns were religious women, similar to nuns although their vows were less strict, who lived in a beguinage. Bruges' Beguinage was founded in 1320, and remained one until recent years before becoming a Benedictine convent, with nuns who 'act' the part of *begijns*. Its charming little whitewashed cottages look out on a wide lawn.
Wijngaardstraat (tel: (050) 330011). Open: the Beguinage courtyard is permanently open. Admission free. Reached by bridge across the canal.

BURG (BURG SQUARE)

An imposing yet charming cobbled square surrounded by monumental buildings which stands at the heart of Bruges' civil and religious life.

Gerechtshof (Court of Justice)

The 18th-century neo-classical palace now houses Bruges' Tourist Office.
Burg 11 (tel: (050) 448686). Open: 1 April to 31 September, Monday to Friday 9.30am–6.30pm, weekends 10am–noon and 2–6.30pm; 1 October to 31 March, Monday to Saturday 9.30am–12.45pm and 2–5.45pm. Admission free.

Baziliek van het Heilig Bloed (Basilica of the Holy Blood)

The Romanesque basilica contains a magnificent gold-and-silver reliquary, inside which is a rock-crystal phial containing a Relic of the Holy Blood, brought to Bruges in 1149 after the Second Crusade by Dirk van de Elzas, the Count of Flanders. The relic is carried in procession each Ascension Day (see page 152).
Burg (tel: (050) 336792). Open: 1 April to 30 September, 9.30am–noon and 2–6pm; 1 October to 31 March, 10am–noon and 2–4pm, closed: Wednesday afternoon. Admission free, but charge for Relic Museum.

Oude Griffie (Old Recorder's House)

In 16th-century Flemish Renaissance-style, this was once the residence of the city's Justice of the Peace.
Burg. Not open to the public.

Proosdij (Deanery)

An ornately decorated, 17th-century baroque building, which was once the palace of the bishops of Bruges.
Burg. Not open to the public.

Stadhuis (City Hall)

A 14th-century Gothic-style construction, whose magnificent Hall is particularly worth visiting for its wall-paintings and wood-vaulted ceiling.
Burg (tel: (050) 448111). Open: 1 April to 31 October, daily 9.30am–5pm; 1 October to 31 March, Monday to Friday 9.30am–12.30pm and 2–5pm. Admission charge.

CANALS

A 40-minute cruise through the canals is one of the city's delights, the impression gained from such a unique angle being unforgettable. There are several landing stages, all of whose boats cover the same sights, from the Begijnhof to Spiegelrei. *Information from Tourist Office (tel: (050)*

448686). Open: 1 March to 31 November, 10am–6pm; December to February only during weekends. Cruise charge. Landing stages at Groene Rei, Rozenhoedkaai and Dijver.

BRUGES

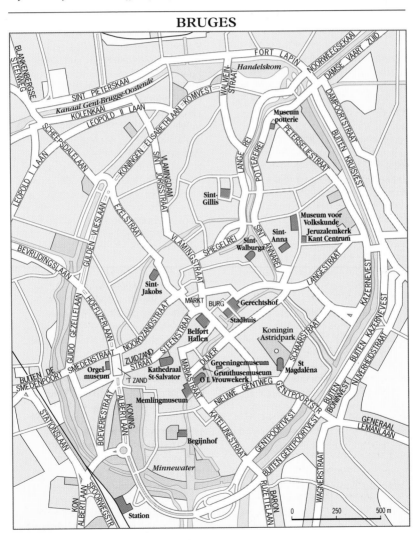

DIJVER

A pretty, tree-lined canal bank between the museums complex and the Burg and Markt squares, where the weekend antiques and flea market is held (see page 144).
This is a continuation of city centre Rozenhoedkaai.

GROENINGEMUSEUM (GROENINGE MUSEUM)

Houses a fine collection of paintings by the 'Flemish Primitives', including Jan Van Eyck, Hans Memling and Rogier van der Weyden. Van Eyck is well represented by his *Madonna with Canon George van der Paele* and a portrait of his wife, *Margerita Van Eyck*. Another stellar work is *The Last Judgement* by Hieronymous Bosch, a gruesome rendering of the horrors awaiting unrepentant sinners.
Dijver 12 (tel: (050) 448750). Open: 1 April to 30 September, daily 9.30am–5pm; 1 October to 31 March, Wednesday to Monday 9.30am–12.30pm and 2–5pm. Admission charge.

GRUUTHUSEMUSEUM (GRUUTHUSE MUSEUM)

Dating from the 15th century, this was the lavish palace of the Lords of Gruuthuse, who owned the monopoly on the sale of *gruut*, a mixture of herbs and spices that went into the making of beer. The palace's fantastic tracery of rose-coloured stone hides an eclectic collection of musical instruments, silks, tapestries, furniture and many *objets d'art*.
Dijver 17 (tel: (050) 448762). Open: 1 April to 30 September, daily 9.30am–5pm; 1 October to 31 March, Wednesday to Monday 9.30am–12.30pm and 2–5pm. Admission charge.

HUIDENVETTERSPLEIN

A trim little square filled with café terraces and a restaurant which used to be the Tanners' Guild House. Popular with street artists.
Between Groene Rei and Rozenhoedkaai.

MARKT (MAIN SQUARE)

Bruges' principal square takes the traditional Flemish form, with guildhouses ranged around it, but instead of a Stadhuis (Town Hall), there is the Provinciaal Hof, the neo-Gothic government building of West Flanders province.

Belfort (Belfry)

Rising from the Hallen (see below), the 79m-high Belfry dominates Bruges. It dates mostly from the 13th century, with the topmost level being a 15th-century addition. Inside, 366 steps lead to a 47-bell carillon served by a full-time carilloneur.

Hallen (Halls)

Begun at the same time as the Belfry, the great market and trading centre of the Halls was continued in various phases during the next 350 years. Interior galleries overlook a courtyard, which used to be a market.
Markt (tel: (050) 405611). Open: 1 April to 30 September, 9.30am–5pm; 1 October to 31 March, 9.30am–12.30pm and 1.30–5pm. Admission charge.

ONZE-LIEVE-VROUWEKERK (CHURCH OF OUR BLESSED LADY)

The 13th-century church, with a 122m-high spire, contains a work of art that has generated a minor tourist industry in its own right: a *Madonna and Child* by Michelangelo, one of the few works by

him to be displayed outside Italy.
*Onze-Lieve-Vrouwekerkhof-Zuid (tel:
(050) 448686). Open: 1 April to 30
September, Monday to Friday 10–11.30am
and 2.30–5pm, Saturday 10–11.30am
and 2.30–4pm, Sunday 2.30am–5pm;
1 October to 31 March, 10–11.30am and
2.30–4.30pm, Saturday 10–11.30am and
2.30–4pm, Sunday 2.30–4.30pm.
Admission charge.*

ROZENHOEDKAAI

Of all the distractingly beautiful views in
Bruges, none surpasses the romantic
outlook from this canalside street, looking
towards the Belfry and the pretty
waterfront buildings and bridges.
*Across the canal from the Burg and Markt
squares.*

SINT-JANSHOSPITAAL (SAINT JOHN'S HOSPITAL)

A 15th-century former hospital is the
unlikely setting for the Hans
Memlingmuseum. One of the 'Flemish
Primitives', Memling was a

Bruges canal-side scene

contemporary of Jan Van Eyck.
*Mariastraat 38 (tel: (050) 448770).
Open: 1 April to 30 September, daily
9.30am–5pm; 1 October to 31 March,
Thursday to Tuesday 9.30am–noon and
2–5pm. Admission charge.*

'T ZAND

Location of Bruges' Saturday-morning
market, this enormous square was once
where the Friday Market was held. 'T
Zand also features a distinctive modern
sculpture group around a fountain.
*On the inner ring road, 500m north of the
railway station.*

VISMARKT (FISH MARKET)

A covered and colonnaded wrought-iron
market dating from 1821, where fish are
sold on most mornings. A particular
delicacy here is raw salted *haring* (herring).
Adjacent to the canal at Groene Rei.

DAMME

A stern-wheel paddle-steamer, the
Lamme Goedzak, leaves from the
jetty at Noorweegse Kaai for a half-
hour cruise along the canal to
Damme, a village which is famed
equally for its intrinsic beauty,
attractive location beside the poplar-
lined canal, windmill and 15th-century
Stadhuis (Town Hall). However, when
all these attractions have been taken
into account, it may still be the many
fine restaurants along the main street,
Kerkstraat, that draws the crowds.
*Located 7km from Bruges, along the
canal to Sluis.*

FLEMISH ART

The revolutionary developments in Flemish art during the late 14th century seemed, like those of its Italian Renaissance counterpart, to spring from thin air. As in Italy, however, they were rooted in the burgeoning wealth of the upper levels of society and in a newly emerging humanist outlook on the world.

Powerful patrons were eager to spend the fruits of the weaving industries in Ghent, Bruges, Ypres and Tournai on the fine things of life, including art. Artists, although still influenced by the formal, stiffly religious Gothic tradition, were ready for something new.

The group that became known as the Flemish 'Primitives' shared a love of nature and of realistic portrayals of humanity's place in the natural world. The greatest name in this group was Jan Van Eyck (c1385–1441), whose luminous use of oils in works like the *Adoration of the Mystic Lamb* (see page 80) and the *Arnolfini Wedding* was a revolutionary development in painting technique.

Other artists are almost equally renowned, contributing to the feeling that 'Primitives' is an inappropriate label. Petrus Christus, Hugo van der Goes, whose *Adoration of the Shepherds* influenced contemporary Italian painters, and Hans Memling, noted for his contemplative portraits, are among the movement's leading lights.

In the hands of Pieter Brueghel the Elder (c1525–69), the Flemish landscape became the setting for gruesome renderings of biblical events and the hard, lusty lives of the peasantry.

By the 17th century, the spotlight had switched from Bruges, Ghent and Brussels to mercantile Antwerp, and the splendour of Pieter-Paul Rubens (1577–1640).

Eight years in Italy added a sensuous touch to Rubens' exuberant style, a characteristic seen in three of his paintings in Antwerp's Cathedral of Our Lady (see page 60): *Raising of the Cross, Descent from the Cross*, and *Resurrection*. Antony Van Dyck and Jacob Jordaens were pupils of Rubens, and continued his tradition.

Above: *The Maids with a Basket of Fruit and Lovers* by Jacob Jordaens

Above: Rubens'
powerful masterpiece,
*The Descent from the
Cross*
Left: the peasants' lusty
lives in Jordaens' *The
King Celebrates*

Taking the sun on the esplanade at Oostende

THE COAST

Belgium has allowed a great deal of unrestrained 'development' on its 70km coastline, with the label 'Atlantic Wall' being attached to the great heaps of concrete and glass that have been thrown up where once there were only sand dunes and an uninterrupted view of the sea.

Nevertheless, the coast retains areas of charm, of open beach, of nature reserve, and of good taste. Elsewhere, a good number of visitors appear to like the bustle, easy access to their hotel or restaurant, and ubiquitous amusement arcades.

DE HAAN

One of the few resorts on the coast that have resisted the temptation to fill themselves up with high-rise apartment blocks. Instead, the belle époque mansions that gave De Haan grace at the turn of the century have been preserved, and fulfil the same pleasant function today.
On the N34 coast road, 12km northeast of Oostende.

DE PANNE

Strong winds and firm sand have made De Panne an ideal location for sand-yachting, both for competitions and fun. *Adjacent to the French border.*

NATUURRESERVAAT HET ZWIN (HET ZWIN NATURE RESERVE)

Belgium's most important nature reserve for birds was formerly an inlet of the North Sea which silted up, creating a tidal wetland that is invaluable for breeding and migrating birds. The reserve covers 150 hectares, 25 of which lie across the Dutch border. More than 100 species of birds, both permanent residents and visitors, can be observed. *Ooievaarslaan 8, Knokke-Heist (tel: (050) 607086). Open: 1 April to 31 September, 9am–7pm; 1 October to 31 March, Thursday to Tuesday 9am–5pm. Admission charge. Past Het Zoute, on Kustlaan and Zwinlaan, towards the Dutch border.*

NATUURRESERVAAT WESTHOEK (WESTHOEK NATURE RESERVE)

The Westhoek covers 340 hectares of

THOMAS COOK'S BELGIUM

In the period between the wars, Thomas Cook promoted holidays from Britain to the Belgian beaches, and especially to Oostende.

protected sand dunes, and gives an idea of how the Belgian coast would have looked in the days before tourism.
De Panne. Open: permanently. Admission free. On the coast, beside the French border.

OOSTENDE
Midway on the Belgian coast, Oostende was one of Europe's classiest 19th-century seaside resorts, having been made fashionable by King Leopold I's decision to establish a holiday residence there. Now more noted as a cross-Channel ferry port, it is still Belgium's busiest beach resort.

James Ensorhuis (James Ensor House)
The Anglo-Belgian artist James Ensor, one of the founders of Expressionism, was born in Oostende. The house where he lived has been transformed into a museum of his life.
Vlaanderenstraat 27 (tel: (059) 805335). Open: 1 June to 30 September, Wednesday to Monday 10am–noon and 2–5pm. Admission charge. Between Wapenplein and the seafront.

Opleidings-Zeilschip *Mercator* (Educational Sailing Ship *Mercator*)
Formerly a merchant navy training ship, the *Mercator*, a graceful, white-painted, three-masted sailing ship, is now a floating maritime museum.

Jachthaven Mercator (tel: (059) 705654). Open: May to September, daily, highly variable schedule: phone first. Admission charge. Opposite railway station.

The shrimp fishermen of Oostduinkerke use horsepower to harvest their catch

PAARDEVISSERS (HORSEBACK FISHERMEN)
Oostduinkerke is an unremarkable seaside resort, except for the Shrimp Fishermen of Oostduinkerke, local men who 'trawl' for shrimp in shallow water just off the beach, using pairs of horses to haul the net. In times past, they were common on the coast, but now only a handful continue the tradition.

On days when they judge the conditions to be favourable, the fishermen take to the water, a remarkable sight in their yellow oilskins, with waves slapping the flanks of their hardy cart-horses. They sell their shrimps to local restaurants, which value their delicate taste.

FLEMISH TOWNS

Flanders' glory lies in its towns and cities, many of which are covered in other parts of this book: Antwerp, Bruges, Ghent, Leuven, Mechelen, Oostende. Smaller towns, however, also have their part to play in the Flemish story.

DIEST

An old fortified city in the east of Flanders, it has a surprising wealth of interest for what is now a small market town. Within the ring of its walls, little has changed in Diest and a stroll round the centre offers something of the historical charm more usually associated with Bruges – although without the canals.

Sint-Sulpitiuskerk (Church of Saint Sulpice)

The church dates from the 14th to 16th centuries; its interior, side chapels and Schatkamer (Treasury) are rich in works of art, including triptychs, sculptures, ornamental tabernacles and a superb baroque organ. *Grote Markt (tel: (013) 312007). Open: 15 May to 15 September, daily 2–5pm. Admission charge for Treasury.*

Stedelijk Museum (Municipal Museum)

Installed in the vaulted cellars of the 18th-century Stadhuis (Town Hall), the museum makes for an atmospheric stroll among finely wrought suits of

Symbol of the cat surmounts Ypres' sumptuous Cloth Hall

medieval armour and other exhibits. *Grote Markt (tel: (013) 312121). Open: 1 January to 31 October, daily 10am–noon and 1–5pm. Admission free.*

IEPER (YPRES)

The history of this 1,000-year-old drapers' town very nearly came to an end in World War I (see pages 88–89 and 90–91). Utterly destroyed then, the town was subsequently rebuilt.

Lakenhalle (Cloth Hall)

This magnificent Gothic extravagance, dating from 1304 and the ultimate symbol of Ypres' weaving-generated wealth, was painstakingly rebuilt after being pounded to dust between 1914 and 1918. The Belfort (Belfry) offers a fine view over Flanders' fields to anyone willing to climb its 264 steps, and there is also a Salient Museum, recalling the four years of dreadful slaughter around Ypres. *Grote Markt (tel: (057) 200724). Open: 1 April to mid-November, daily 9.30am–noon and 1.30–5.30pm, closed Monday. Admission charge.*

Hotel-Museum Merghelynck (Merghelynck Museum)

Established in a patrician town house from 1744, this fine-arts museum features a notable collection of furniture, jewellery and

Chinese and Japanese porcelain.
*Merghelynckstraat 2 (tel: (057) 203042).
Open: Monday to Saturday 10am–noon
and 2–5pm for guided tours only.
Admission charge.*

KORTRIJK (COURTRAI)

An emblematic event in Flemish history
took place here: the Battle of the Golden
Spurs, on 11 July 1302. A force of
Flemish peasants, struggling for
independence from France, destroyed an
army composed of the flower of French
chivalry. After the battle, the victorious
Flemish collected over 700 knights' spurs
and hung them as a symbol of triumph.

Begijnhof (Beguinage)

Founded in 1238, although the flower-
bedecked courtyard of small white
houses with red-tiled roofs dates from
the 17th century. It is overlooked by the
soaring Gothic belfry of nearby Sint-
Maartenskerk (Saint Martin's Church).
*Begijnhofstraat. Located 100m from the
Grote Markt. People live in the houses.*

OUDENAARDE

Originally a centre of the cloth industry,
Oudenaarde became famous for
tapestry-making in the 15th century,
when its wares were prized by courts
and kings throughout Europe.

Stadhuis (Town Hall)

The delicate tracery of this flamboyant
example of 16th-century Flemish Gothic
is well worth seeing, as is the adjoining
13th-century Lakenhalle (Cloth Hall).
*Grote Markt (tel: (055) 317251). Open:
1 April to 31 October, weekends 2–5pm,
guided tours only. Admission charge.*

VEURNE (FURNES)

Situated in the polderland some 6km

Main Square in Veurne, one of Flanders' finest
and most atmospheric

behind the coast, Veurne was a Spanish
garrison town under the Habsburg
Empire.

Grote Markt (Main Square)

Veurne is particularly noted for this
17th-century square, one of Belgium's
most perfect Flemish Renaissance
ensembles.

Stadhuis (Town Hall)

An ornate, blue-and-gold embellished
loggia stands out from the façade, and a
museum inside features leather wall-
hangings from Córdoba and Mechelen.
*Grote Markt (tel: (058) 312154). Open: for
guided tours only, 1 April to 30 September,
daily 11am, 2pm, 3pm, 4.30pm; 1 October
to 31 March on request. Admission charge.*

Sint-Walburgakerk (Saint Walburga's Church)

An imposing 13th-century church, focus
of Veurne's renowned *Boetprocessie*
(Procession of the Penitents: see page
152).
*Sint-Walburgapark (tel: (058) 312198).
Open: Easter to 31 October, daily
10am–noon and 3–6pm. Admission free.
Adjacent to the Grote Markt.*

At Bokrijk's Open-air Museum, the past is brought back to life

DE KEMPEN (THE KEMPEN)

A great expanse of heathland to the east of Antwerp, along the border with Holland, the Kempen is rough open countryside crossed by streams and canals, and dotted with lakes.

Once well-nigh inaccessible, the Kempen is now popular with tourists for its nature reserves, camping grounds, tranquil villages and abbeys.

BAARLE-HERTOG

This village is a geographical curiosity, being a Belgian village in the Netherlands, adjacent to Dutch Baarle-Nassau.
Located 14km north of Turnhout.

BOBBEJAANLAND

Theme park (see page 156).

DOMEIN BOKRIJK (BOKRIJK ESTATE)

Incorporates an Openluchtmuseum (Open-air Museum), dedicated to the historic way of life in Flanders. Long-abandoned crafts are presented in farms, windmills and cottages by people wearing traditional costume, while demonstrations of traditional sports show that recreation is no new concept.
Provinciaal Domein Bokrijk (tel: (011) 224575). Open: park all year; museum 4 April to 1 November, daily 10am–6pm. Admission charge. Between Hasselt and Genk, 2km from the N75.

LANDCOMMANDERIJ ALDEN BIESEN (ALDEN BIESEN CASTLE)

Eight centuries old, Alden Biesen was a 'commandery' of the Teutonic Knights. The dramatic structure is now a museum and international centre for tourism and the arts. Its towers and walls are reached by crossing a moat, and there are ornamental gardens, a chapel and extensive outbuildings.
Kasteelstraat 6, Bilzen-Rijkhoven (tel: (089) 417033). Open: daily 10am–6pm. Admission charge. Exit 31 from E313.

NATIONAAL JENEVERMUSEUM (NATIONAL GENEVA MUSEUM)

Based in Hasselt, the centre of Belgium's *geneva* (gin) industry, the museum celebrates a drink which rivals beer as the national beverage (see page 173). A taste of the finished product rounds off a stroll through exhibits of distillation equipment, bottles, labels and other mementoes.
Witte Nonnenstraat 19, Hasselt (tel: (011) 241144). Open: Tuesday to Friday 10am–5pm, weekends 2–6pm. Closed Monday. Admission charge. Town centre.

TONGEREN (TONGRES)

Ambiorix, leader of the Belgian revolt against Julius Caesar, defeated two Roman legions here and is honoured by a statue in the Grote Markt.

Onze-Lieve-Vrouwebasiliek (Basilica of Our Lady)

The 13th- to 15th-century Basilica is richly ornamented, while its Schatkamer (Treasury) contains memorable pieces, including a 12th-century Head of Christ and the 13th-century Shrine of the Martyrs of Trier.
Grote Markt (tel: (012) 232164). Open: May to September, 10am–noon, 1.30–5pm; October to April, upon request. Admission charge for Treasury.

Provinciaal Gallo-Romeinsmuseum (Provincial Gallo-Roman Museum)

Houses archaeological finds, including coins, maps and road-markers from the days of Ambiorix and Julius Caesar.
Kielenstraat 15 (tel: (012) 233914). Open: Tuesday, Friday and Sunday 10am–6pm, Monday noon–6pm, Wednesday and Thursday 10am–9pm. Admission charge. Behind the Basilica.

TURNHOUT

Belgium's northernmost town. Playing cards are manufactured here.

Nationaal Museum van de Speelkaart (National Playing Cards Museum)

Playing cards were once produced in the Mesmaekers factory, now a museum.
Druivenstraat 18 (tel: (014) 415621). Open: 1 June to 31 August, Tuesday to Saturday 2–5pm, Sunday 10am–noon and 2–5pm; 1 September to 31 May, Wednesday, Friday and Saturday 2–5pm, Sunday 10am–noon and 2–5pm.

A carpet of flowers fills Tongeren's Main Square with colour and scent

Admission charge. Located 100m from the Grote Markt.

Taxandriamuseum (Taxandria Museum)

Taxandria was the Roman name for the Kempen, and the museum features archaeological finds from the area from prehistoric to Merovingian times.
Begijnenstraat 28 (tel: (014) 436335). Open: opening times may change due to rebuilding, phone first. Admission charge. Located 100m east of Grote Markt.

ZILVERMEER (SILVER LAKE)

In the Kempen's lake district, this is a miniature 'inland seaside resort'.
Domein Zilvermeer, Mol (tel: (014) 816021). Open: all year from dawn to sunset. Admission charge. Located 12km from Mol via the N74 and N712.

GENT/GAND (GHENT)

Ghent, an inland port on the River Scheldt, shares some characteristics with Bruges (see pages 66–9), but feels more like a real city, a lived-in place. The city is generally considered to be the heartland of Flemish culture (though not without some opposition from other contenders for this title).

It has areas of industrial blight, particularly along the outlying canals. In the old centre, however, are reminders of the medieval mercantile and weaving traditions that brought the city wealth, and of the Counts of Flanders whose capital it was.

BELFORT (BELFRY) AND LAKENHALLE (CLOTH HALL)

A complex of 13th- and 14th-century buildings, of which the 90m-high Belfry offers a superb view over the city. The ostentatious Cloth Hall includes an 18th-century prison, source of the

The Korenlei (Corn Quay) – a favourite location for scenic picture-taking

legend of the Mammelokker, a young woman whose imprisoned father was starving to death. She supposedly breast-fed him through the bars, hearing which the authorities freed him.
Sint-Baafsplein (tel: (09) 225 9105).
Open: 1 April to 31 October, Tuesday to Sunday 9.30am–6pm; 1 November to 31 March, 9.30am–4.30pm. Admission charge.

GRAVENSTEEN (CASTLE OF THE COUNTS)

A bleak fortress, dating from 1180. The castle dominates its surroundings but gave up its military role in the 14th century, being used later as a mint, court, gaol and cotton mill. It is as a castle, however, that it is best recalled, complete with torture room and ramparts from where crossbow bolts and boiling oil were poured on attackers.
Sint-Veerleplein (tel: (09) 225 9306).
Open: 1 April to 30 September, 9am–6pm; 1 October to 31 March, 9am–5pm. Admission charge. Hoogpoort and the River Leie.

HET PAND

A former Dominican abbey on the banks of the Leie, transformed into a cultural complex of offices and studios. A visit gives some idea of the monks' habitat oddly juxtaposed with its contemporary use.
Onderbergen 1. Open: office hours. Admission free. Only public areas are normally accessible. Just south of Saint Michael's Church.

KORENLEI (CORN QUAY)

Korenlei is a favourite place for taking that one picture which aims to capture the essence of Ghent in a single frame, especially when sunlight reflects the gabled guild-houses on the River Leie. This and the facing Graslei was the heart of the medieval port. The guild-houses display several gable styles and decoration, but the ensemble is satisfying enough just for its romantic atmosphere. City boat tours leave from here.
Adjacent to Sint-Michielsbrug (Saint Michael's Bridge).

MUSEUM VOOR SIERKUNST (DECORATIVE ARTS MUSEUM)

This graceful old museum, constructed around a villa with a central courtyard, offers two distinct faces of the decorative arts, the old and the new. Period rooms and collections of old porcelain predominate, while the modern section offers the sometimes weird-and-wonderful products of late 20th-century design.
Jan Breydelstraat 5 (tel: (09) 225 6676). Open: Tuesday to Sunday 9.30am–5pm. Admission charge. Located 50m north of Korenlei.

MUSEUM VOOR VOLKSKUNDE (FOLKLORE MUSEUM)

Founded in what used to be a courtyard complex of alms houses, the Folklore

The medieval centre of Ghent is renowned for its many fine churches

Museum features a time in Ghent's history that it is almost contemporary: the turn of the century. The alms houses, which are much older, have been converted into a series of rooms and workshops aiming to give an idea of how people lived then.
Kraanlei 65 (tel: (09) 223 1336). Open: 1 April to 2 November, daily, 9am–12.30pm and 1.30–5.30pm; 3 November to 31 March, daily 10am–noon and 1.30–5pm. Admission charge. Kraanlei begins opposite the entrance to the Gravensteen.

PATERSHOL

A jumble of narrow streets and medieval houses, many of which have a new function as restaurants and bars and are a favourite haunt of Ghentenaars out for the evening.
Begins opposite the entrance to the Gravensteen, between Geldmunt and Kraanlei.

SINT-BAAFSKATHEDRAAL (SAINT BAVO'S CATHEDRAL)

An awesomely magnificent Gothic construction, eloquent testimony to the richness of Ghent during its medieval and Renaissance heyday when the cloth trade placed it among Europe's most important cities.

There is a curious mismatch between the bare stone walls and the marble ornamentation added in later years. The marble and oak pulpit, reminiscent of Bernini, is typical of the cathedral's slightly conceited style; Ghent moved in the same cultural circles as Florence, far ahead of other European cities in its day. The ornate guild chapels and magnificent altar add to this impression.

Pride of place goes to the triptych by Jan Van Eyck, the *Adoration of the Mystic Lamb,* one of the great works of European art, considering the realism of its representation of nature and of its figures, including Christ, the Virgin and Saint John.

Sint-Baafsplein (tel: (09) 223 1046). Open: summer – daily 9.30am–noon, 2–6pm, Sunday 1–6pm; winter – daily 10.30am–noon, 2.30–4pm, Sunday 2–5pm. Free, but admission charge to see the Adoration of the Mystic Lamb. *Across Goudenleeuwplein from the Town Hall.*

SINT-MICHIELSKERK (SAINT MICHAEL'S CHURCH)

Another of Ghent's three most outstanding medieval churches, Saint Michael's contains important religious paintings and sculptures, including *Christ Dying on the Cross* by Antony Van Dyck.

Sint-Michielstraat (tel: (09) 225 8805). Open: generally only during services. Admission free. Beside Sint-Michielsbrug.

SINT-NIKLAASKERK (SAINT NICHOLAS' CHURCH)

The third of Ghent's trinity of splendid city-centre churches, and the foremost example of the Scheldt Gothic style in Belgium. It dates fron the 13th century and has a richly embellished interior. *Korenmarkt (tel: (09) 225 9464). Open: daily 9am–noon, 2–5pm. Admission free.*

SCHOOLMUSEUM MICHEL THIERY (MICHEL THIERY SCHOOL MUSEUM)

The museum includes a fascinating scale-model of Ghent during the reign of the 16th-century Habsburg Emperor Charles V, with an accompanying sound-and-light show.

Sint-Pietersplein 14 (tel: (09) 222 8050. Open: Monday to Thursday and Saturday 9am–12.15pm and 1.30–5.15pm, Friday 9am–12.15pm, closed Sunday. Admission charge. In Sint-Pietersabdij (Saint Peter's Abbey) south of the city centre.

STADHUIS (TOWN HALL)

Built in four stages, the Town Hall ranges from 15th-century late Gothic to 18th-century baroque. There is public access by guided tour to several of its magnificently decorated halls, including the Pacificatiezaal.

Botermarkt (tel: (09) 241555). Open: May to October, Monday to Thursday 2–5pm, guided tours only. Across the square from Saint Bavo's Cathedral.

Tourist information about Ghent and events taking place in the city is available from Infokantoor, Dienst Toerisme van Gent, Stadhuis, Botermarkt, B-9000 Ghent *(tel: (09) 266 5232 or 224 1555). Open: April to November, daily 9.30am–6.30pm; November to March, daily 9.30am–4.30pm.*

Set in the countryside near Ghent, Ooidonk Castle is one of Belgium's finest fortresses

AROUND GHENT

KASTEEL OOIDONK (OOIDONK CASTLE)

A fine moated 16th-century château with onion-shaped turreted towers, rather incongruously situated in an area of traditional red-and-white-painted farmhouses.

Ooidonkdreef, Deurle (tel: (09) 282 3570). Open: Easter to 15 September, Sunday and public holidays (also Saturday in July and August), 2–5.30pm. Admission charge. Ten kilometres southwest of Ghent on the N43.

DONKMEER

A lake that has developed as a day-trip and weekend-break centre, with small boats for hire, cafés and restaurants.
At Berlare, 12km east of Ghent on the N443.

SINT-MARTENS-LATEM

The old riverside village of Sint-Martens-Latem retains much of its charm, as well as its reputation as a 'village of artists'. There are many private galleries in the village.
By the River Leie, 10km southwest of Ghent.

Oostende · Brugge ■ Antwerpen
Gent ·
Ieper · ■ Bruxelles/
Brussel · Eupen
Namur ■
Spa

Brugge (Bruges) City Centre Walk

Bruges is such a stunningly well-preserved city (see pages 66–9), its architecture dating from medieval times onwards, that it sometimes has the air of a film set or as if it has been specially treated to preserve the graces of a bygone era. *Allow 4 hours for the walk.*

If time allows, the walk should ideally be preceded by a boat-trip through the network of canals. This gives a fascinating view of the city from a unique perspective and should add to the interest of the walk, which begins in the Markt (Main Square).

1 MARKT

A superbly atmospheric square, with medieval banners floating from its gabled buildings, and dominated by the 79m-high Belfort (Belfry) of the Hallen, whose 47-bell carillon breaks into song at every opportunity. Below the Belfry are the Hallen, once used for fairs. The nearby, ornate Provinciaal Hof houses the West Flanders provincial government.

Take Breidelstraat, at the side of the Hallen, to Bruges's most historic square.

2 BURG (BURG SQUARE)

Together in this small space are magnificent buildings that span the centuries from the 14th to the 19th. Pride of place belongs to the Romanesque Heilig Bloed Baziliek (Basilica of the Holy Blood), which contains a much-venerated Relic of the Holy Blood. The Stadhuis (Town Hall) dates from the 14th century, in Gothic style. Other notable buildings are the 16th-century Flemish Renaissance-style Oude Griffie (Old Recorders' House), the 17th-century baroque Proosdij

(Deanery) and the 18th-century neo-classical Gerechtshof (Court of Justice). *Take narrow Blinde-Ezelstraat and cross the canal bridge, and turn left once across.*

3 VISMARKT (FISH MARKET)

Fish are still sold on most mornings in the colonnaded arcade of the Fish Market, which dates from 1821. *Retrace your steps past the bridge to Huidenvettersplein, and past Landing Stage 1, one of the places from which the canal boat-trips leave.*

Rest and relaxation are easily achieved at Bruges' Beguinage

4 HUIDENVETTERSPLEIN

This atmospheric little square is surrounded by café terraces and restaurants, one of which used to be the Tanners' Guild House. Street artists congregate here in good weather to sketch customers sunning themselves on the terraces. *Continue on to Rozenhoedkaai, which has a fine view over the canal of the old canalside houses and the Belfry, until you arrive at the Dijver, a tree-shaded bank where the weekend antiques and flea market is held. Turn left for the Groeningemuseum.*

5 GROENINGEMUSEUM (GROENINGE MUSEUM)

The Fine Arts Museum at No 12 houses an important collection of works by the so-called 'Flemish Primitives', including Jan van Eyck, Hans Memling and Rogier van der Weyden. *Returning to the Dijver, take Gruuthusestraat, then the little alleyway on the left that leads to a small courtyard.*

6 GRUUTHUSEMUSEUM (GRUUTHUSE MUSEUM)

At the far end of the courtyard is the fairy-tale edifice of the Gruuthusemuseum. In the 15th century, this was the palace of the Lords of Gruuthuse, a family which had the monopoly on the sale of *gruut*, a herbs-and-spices mixture for improving the taste of beer. *The courtyard ends in a grove of lime trees. Pass through this and the narrow alleyway at the side of the palace.*

7 ONZE-LIEVE-VROUWEKERK (CHURCH OF OUR BLESSED LADY)

Inside the church, behind protective glass, is a *Madonna and Child* by Michelangelo, one of the few works by the Renaissance master outside Italy. The Carrara marble sculpture is surprisingly small compared with how it looks in photographs, but it is spellbindingly beautiful. *Come out on to Katelijnestraat, and walk down the road before turning right into Stoofstraat, then cross Walplein, turn right into Wijngaardstraat and cross over the bridge.*

8 BEGIJNHOF (BEGUINAGE)

Founded in the 13th century, this charming courtyard of small almshouses functioned until recent times as a home for *begijns*, religious lay women akin to nuns. The Begijnhof is now a Benedictine convent.

The Coast Tram

While there are other ways of travelling the 70km-long Belgian coastline (see pages 72–3), many people take advantage of a special mode of transport. The Kusttram (Coast Tram) traverses the coast from the Dutch border to the French and back again, stopping at all the towns and villages along the way and at many points between. *Allow 2 hours for the run.*

The route is from Knokke to De Panne. If you arrive at Knokke by car, remember to add 2 hours for getting back. If arriving by train, you can begin at Knokke, complete the trip to De Panne and return by train from Oostende.

KNOKKE–HEIST
The ritziest resort on the coast. The tram begins in front of Knokke railway station and runs through the residential and shopping district before reaching the seafront just as the beaches of Heist are giving way to Zeebrugge.
From Knokke–Heist to Zeebrugge takes 14 minutes.

ZEEBRUGGE
Although not especially attractive, Zeebrugge is Belgium's main North Sea port and presumably is compensated by wealth-creation. The tram passes over the Leopoldkanaal (Leopold Canal) from Holland and the Boudewijnkanaal (Baudouin Canal) from Bruges. Beyond Zeebrugge it runs along the shore for a few kilometres before swinging inland to Blankenberge.
From Zeebrugge to Blankenberge takes 8 minutes.

BLANKENBERGE
Although missing Blankenberge's

De Haan's fine legacy of belle époque mansions makes it the jewel of the coast

Kursaal casino (which is on the seafront) the tram arrives by the waterside at the harbour, with its lighthouse and yacht clubs. It then squeezes between the dunes and the camping sites at Harendijke, before Wenduine and the Duinenreservaat Zandpanne (Zandpanne Dunes Reserve), to De Haan.
From Blankenberge to De Haan takes 16 minutes.

DE HAAN

This small resort is the jewel of the coast, having avoided the overbuilding of apartment blocks and hotels that has spoiled others. De Haan's elegant belle époque mansions delight the eye on the tram's route through, while the green of golf-courses continues the relaxed atmosphere beyond the town. From here to Bredene-aan-Zee the route is along the seafront until Oostende is reached.
From De Haan to Oostende takes 18 minutes.

OOSTENDE

The second busiest port, although mainly for ferry traffic and fishing boats, Oostende has grown from a 19th-century royal resort to a small city. The tram makes a wide detour around its yacht-jammed harbour, side stepping the busy Visserskaai (Fishermen's Wharf) before arriving at the Coast Tram terminal beside the railway station. Then it is through town towards the Kursaal casino, reaching the seafront at Mariakerke-Bad and running straight along beside the water. On the other side are dunes studded with World War II German coastal defence bunkers. It bids farewell to the seaview by turning away at Westende, on the

inland stretch towards Nieuwpoort.
From Oostende to Nieuwpoort takes 38 minutes.

NIEUWPOORT

Belgium's premier fishing port, Nieuwpoort lives up to its reputation for fine seafood in the long line of fishmongers that flanks the harbour. An equestrian statue of the World War I King Albert stands where the line crosses the yacht harbour channel. The tram reaches the seafront dunes again at Oostduinkerke (where you might spot the Shrimp Fishermen of Oostduinkerke working the waves on their horses) and continues through them, arriving at an increasingly built-up area, crossing the empty Natuurreservaat De Doornpanne (De Doornpanne Nature Reserve), and on through Koksijde to De Panne.
From Nieuwpoort to De Panne takes 26 minutes.

The wide, sandy beach at De Panne

DE PANNE

The tram-line ends a few minutes' walk from the shore-front monument to the first King of the Belgians, Leopold I, and the beach where sand-yachts make their exhilarating runs in blustery weather.

Gent (Ghent) City Centre Walk

Ghent has a compact city centre (see pages 78–81), and most of its interesting places are within easy walking distance. This makes the walk a fine introduction to Ghent's historic treasures. *Allow 4 hours.*

Begin at the Korenmarkt. You can nourish yourself for the 4-hour walk with an oliebol *(a kind of doughnut) at the fairground-style pavement diner. Then take the adjacent street, Klein Turkije.*

1 SINT-NIKLAASKERK (CHURCH OF SAINT NICHOLAS)

Although undergoing a long-term process of reconstruction,

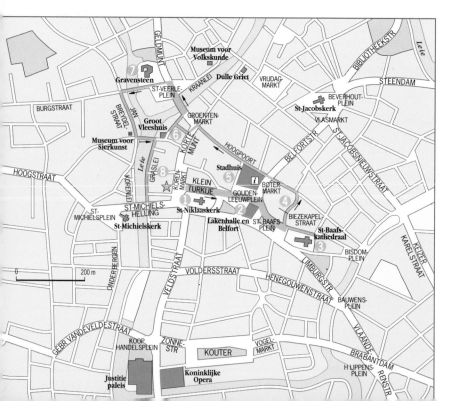

the church's exterior of grey stone, in Flemish Gothic style, is a good example of the religious edifices that dominate Ghent's skyline. It should be possible to get at least a peek at the enormous interior.

Continue 100m to a square called Goudenleeuwplein.

2 LAKENHALLE (CLOTH HALL) AND BELFORT (BELFRY)

The Cloth Hall and the Belfry form a complex of 14th- and 13th-century buildings at the facing end of Goudenleeuwplein, which is dominated by the Belfry's 90m-high tower. You may be lucky enough to hear its carillon tinkling over atmospheric Goudenleeuwplein as you cross.

Ghent is a city of towers, the next one being across Sint-Baafsplein.

3 SINT-BAAFSKATHEDRAAL (SAINT BAVO'S CATHEDRAL)

You should be well into the medieval and Renaissance spirit by now, your sense of time nudged out of joint by the surroundings. Saint Bavo's takes the process a step further. One of Europe's great cathedrals, holding 700 years of history within its walls, it also contains Jan Van Eyck's the *Adoration of the Mystic Lamb.*

Go right outside the cathedral, to adjacent Biezekapelstraat.

4 BIEZEKAPELSTRAAT

Often used as a period set in Belgian film and television productions, this narrow, Z-shaped cobbled street acts like a time machine. Old houses stand side by side with a convent, the courtyard of Ghent's 14th-century Koninklijk Muziekconservatorium (Royal Conservatory of Music) and a

shrine containing a Madonna and Child. *Turn left on to Hoogpoort, passing the magnificent old Sint-Jorishof Hotel, then cross Botermarkt to the continuation of Hoogpoort.*

5 STADHUIS (TOWN HALL)

The façade of the Town Hall along Hoogpoort (see page 81) is the most spectacular section as well as being easily observed because the street is fairly quiet.

Cross the Korte Munt square.

6 GROOT VLEESHUIS (MAIN MEAT MARKET)

In the Middle Ages, the Meat Market must have been a fascinating, if probably appalling, place. Today its dingy grey stone blocks still conjure up the difficult life and times of the people in those days, although meat is no longer sold there.

Cross the bridge over the Leie to Sint-Veerleplein.

7 GRAVENSTEEN (CASTLE OF THE COUNTS)

This dark and mysterious castle shows none of the grace inherent in most of Ghent's historic buildings. The message here was one of power and it must have been received loud and clear.

Go left on Sint-Veerleplein, cross the bridge, turn left on to Jan Breydelstraat, and left again, over the bridge. Turn right, along Graslei.

8 GRASLEI

Graslei is the bank of the Leie opposite Korenlei, and contains the finest guild houses as well as the medieval Tolhuisje (Toll House), now a bar.

At the end of Graslei, climb the steps to Sint-Michiels.

IN FLANDERS' FIELDS

'Old soldiers never die, they just fade away.' As the survivors of the madness that was once called simply the 'Great War' fade away, a terrible knowledge is fading with them: the reality of a war so dreadful that people comforted themselves by saying it would be 'the war to end all wars'.

We know better now, but we will never know more than the palest shadow of an answer to the question: 'What was World War I really like?'. On any day between 1914 and 1918, any soldier, Allied or German, taking the shell-swept roads around the Flemish town of Ieper (Ypres: see pages 74 and 90–1) and turning off to their designated stretch of trenches, would count themselves fortunate to survive the journey.

Once at their little piece of the muddy, waterlogged Western Front, for 24 hours every day, they would live on a diet of fear and boredom. Snipers, artillery shells, mortars, hand-grenades, poison gas, flame-throwers, bayonets and clubbed rifles would do their best to end the misery. Always, there would be cold, dirt, lice, rain, and despair that the nightmare would ever end.

At frequent intervals, the generals would draw arrows on

Little remains of the battlefield, but there are some trenches, and many memorials

their maps, and set objectives, and issue orders. The artillery would roar for a month or more. Finally, a whistle would blow, and young men from Saskatchewan or Stuttgart or Stafford would clamber over the top of their trench and walk towards the waiting rifles and machine-guns.

'For by my glee might many men have laughed,
And of my weeping something had been left,
Which must die now. I mean the truth untold,
The pity of war…'
Wilfred Owen, 1893–1918

Wilfred Owen was killed in action one week before the Armistice.
Today, it is all quiet on the Western Front, but the pity of war still haunts Flanders' fields, and the poppies that bloom in wild profusion each spring seem like nature's silent tribute to the fallen.

Ieper (Ypres)
Battlefield

The British Tommies solved the problem of how
to pronounce Ypres (Ieper in Dutch), in their own
inimitable way. 'Wipers', they called it, and the
name had a certain grim symbolism, given the
events that took place here between 1914 and
1918 (see pages 74 and 88–9).

Little remains of the great battlefield itself, but there
are monuments, 170 military cemeteries, old pillboxes
and a preserved stretch of trenches. There are also
unexploded shells uprooted by farmers. This 'harvest of
death' still claims lives and such items should not be
touched. *Allow half a day for this drive through the
Ypres Salient.*

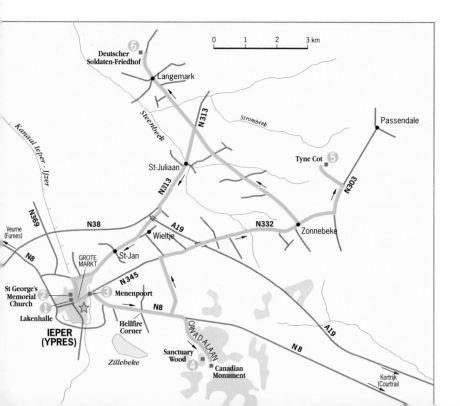

Begin in the Grote Markt (Main Square) in Ypres, and try to picture this handsome town as a flattened, reeking ruin. The first two locations are reached on foot.

1 LAKENHALLE (CLOTH HALL)

Painstakingly restored, the Gothic Cloth Hall that dominates the Grote Markt was a symbol of the wealth created by Ypres' medieval weaving industry. Today it houses the Salient Museum, which gives an idea of the events of those four dreadful years.

From the Salient Museum, turn left on to Coomansstraat and cross Vandenpeereboomplein to the corner of Elverdingsestraat.

2 SAINT GEORGE'S MEMORIAL CHURCH

Completed in 1929, the church is a treasure-trove of mementoes of the British and Commonwealth forces who fought in the Ypres Salient, and memories of the many who fell.

From here, return to the Grote Markt, collect your car and leave the town by Meensestraat.

3 MENENPOORT (MENEN GATE)

A neo-classical marble portico spanning the gateway through Ieper's 17th-century defensive wall. Carved on the white expanse of stone are the names of some 56,000 soldiers with no known grave. Every evening at 8 o'clock, members of the Ypres Fire Brigade sound the Last Post in a short but moving ceremony.

Continue on Meensestraat, which becomes the N8 as it leaves town, past 'Hellfire Corner'. Turn right after 3km, on to Canadalaan, following the signs for 'Hill 62' and 'Sanctuary Wood'.

4 SANCTUARY WOOD

A stretch of waterlogged trenches, pocked with shell holes and dotted with shattered trees, which gives a few pale answers to the inevitable question: What was it really like? Access is via the Sanctuary Wood Museum attached to a café. A little further along Canadalaan is the Canadian Monument on Hill 62.

Return to the N8, turn left, then immediately right. At a T-junction adjacent to two military cemeteries, turn right following the sign for Zonnebeke. One kilometre after Zonnebeke, go left on the N303 towards Passendale (Passchendaele) for 1km, then left to Tyne Cot.

5 TYNE COT MILITARY CEMETERY

The biggest Commonwealth cemetery in the Ypres Salient, with nearly 12,000 graves, Tyne Cot is a place of great calm and some beauty, with its Cross of Remembrance in white Portland stone built over the remains of a concrete bunker. Most of the soldiers here died in the Battle of Passchendaele in 1917.

Return to Zonnebeke, go right at the village crossroads, 6km to Langemark, and carry straight on for 1km.

6 DEUTSCHER SOLDATEN-FRIEDHOF (GERMAN SOLDIERS CEMETERY)

With 44,000 burials, the cemetery is a reminder that the sufferings of war visited both sides in equal measure. Many of the soldiers here were young members of the Student Regiments who marched off towards slaughter in 1914 in what was called the 'Massacre of the Innocents'.

Return to Langemark and take the road towards Zonnebeke. At the junction with the N313, turn right to return to Ypres.

Wallonie (Wallonia)

*W*ith some 3.2 million inhabitants, the region of Wallonia covers most of the French-speaking part of Belgium (although some of its population continues to speak the ancient dialect called Walloon), while a small number, some 67,000, living in the East Cantons speak German (see pages 100–3).

Wallonia broadly comprises the southern half of Belgium, including the southern half of Brabant, Brabant-Wallon Province, and all of the provinces of Hainaut, Liège, Namur and Luxembourg (not to be confused with the neighbouring Grand Duchy of Luxembourg). In the various reorganisations of the Belgian state, it has been given wide powers of autonomy over economic, social and cultural affairs. The regional capital is Namur, a resort town on the River Meuse (see pages 112–13).

Although it seems now to be a logical whole, Wallonia is a recent and relatively artificial construction. It was a 19th-century poet, Grandgagnage, who coined the name as a cultural counterweight to the historical resonance of Flanders.

Undoubtedly the most important rulers were the Prince-Bishops of Liège, who, between the 10th and 15th centuries, wielded both political and ecclesiastic power over the territory around Liège. They came into conflict with other local potentates, such as the Counts of Namur, and were finally overwhelmed by outside forces. Tournai has also known the attractions of power, having been a kind of 5th-century Capital of Europe as the seat of the Frankish Empire in the days of King Clovis.

In more recent times, Liège and its rival Charleroi have been the centres of economic power, a power that was based on the old industries of coal, steel and heavy manufacturing and which has faded as those industries declined. Nowadays, with Flanders ahead in the 'sunrise' industries, Wallonia is trying to reinvent itself economically by attracting

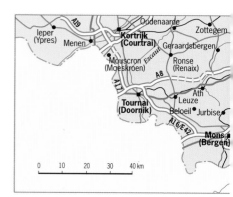

the high-technology industries and services it needs in the 21st century.

Land for tourists
One prime asset that Wallonia has in what is the most important service sector – tourism – lies in the ancient hills and forests of the Ardennes. This product of the glaciers is often thought to comprise all of Wallonia but in fact represents the area between the River Meuse and the German border, although there is no precise definition as it is a geographical concept rather than a political entity.

The sparsely populated Ardennes rivals the Flemish coast as Belgium's premier tourist destination.

In addition, there is the scenic valley and the resort towns of the River Meuse; the art cities of Tournai and Liège; the rivers, rolling countryside and abbeys of Hainaut; and the high, rugged plateau of the Hautes Fagnes (which lie within the East Cantons). Folklore and carnival are important aspects of life here, with outbursts of good-natured mayhem breaking out in the most seemingly sober-sided villages at some specially selected time of the year (see pages 152–3).

Wallonia also has a well-deserved reputation for the range and quality of its cuisine. Gastronomic weekends are a favourite kind of break, especially for jaded palates from the big cities during the autumn and winter game season, when wild boar, pheasant, hare and venison in abundance find themselves in hunters' sights and on restaurant menus.

With the great outdoors right on its doorstep, Wallonia seems fit for anything.

WALLONIA

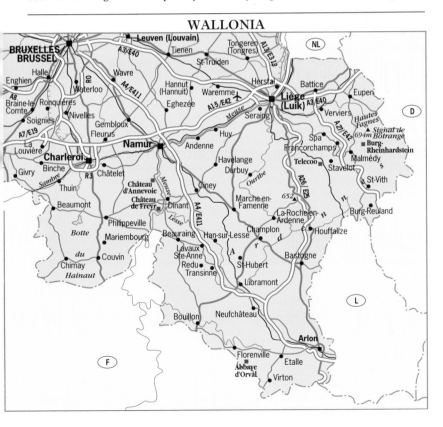

THE ARDENNES

An area of hills, forests, and steep river valleys covering much of Wallonia, the Ardennes is Belgium's scenic treasure. Here, you are caught up in the activities of the countryside – farming, forestry, hunting, fishing.

There is no 'bad' time to visit the Ardennes. The seasons unfold at nature's leisurely pace and life slows down to match them. In spring the landscape is bright with the fresh promise of the reawakening land; summer raises the Ardennes' holiday-playground character to its height; in autumn the forests are a blaze of reds, browns and golds; and winter sees cross-country skis unloaded from their racks.

Although the Ardennes has no shortage of individual places of interest, many of them listed below, it is the region as a whole that attracts. Simply walking, cycling or driving around, aimlessly even, is at least as satisfying as following a plan to 'see everything'.

ABBAYE D'ORVAL (ORVAL ABBEY)

A medieval abbey that has experienced most of the trials and tribulations of changing political and religious fashions. A modern Trappist monastery occupies the site beside a former Cistercian foundation which has been destroyed regularly over the centuries. The abbey is renowned for its beer and cheese.
Villers-devant-Orval (tel: (061) 311060). Ruins open: Sunday between Easter and end September, 9.30am–12.30pm and 1.30–6.30pm; Sunday between October and Easter, 10am–12.30pm and 1.30–5.30pm. Admission charge. Located 1km from the N88 southeast of Florenville.

ARLON

One of Belgium's main towns in Roman times, and which retains vestiges from those days, Arlon is built on a hilltop near the Luxembourg border, with a fine view from the belfry of the Eglise Saint-Donat (Church of Saint Donat) over the surrounding countryside.

Musée Luxembourgeois

Conserves valuable remnants from Luxembourg province's Roman past, including a notable collection of funerary monuments and other sculpture, as well as objects from the earlier Gallic and later Frankish periods.
Rue des Martyrs 13 (tel: (063) 221236). Open: Monday to Saturday 9am–noon and 2–5pm. Admission charge.

BASTOGNE

The town is a modern reconstruction, having been virtually destroyed during the Ardennes Offensive of 1944 (see page 99). 'Nuts' was the succinct reply of American General Anthony MacAuliffe to a German surrender demand, and the town saw some of the bitterest fighting of that dreadful winter conflict.

Mardasson Monument

An imposing, star-shaped memorial to the Americans who fell in the battle, with inscriptions recording the units involved. In the adjacent Bastogne Historical Centre, an audio-visual presentation, whose script was prepared by General MacAuliffe and his opponent, General Hasso von Manteuffel, provides detailed information on the action.
Colline du Mardasson (Mardasson Hill) (tel: (061) 211413). Open: 1 March to 30 April and 1 October to 15 November,

Mist rising from the River Ourthe wafts over the pretty village of Durbuy

*10am–4pm; May, June and September,
9.30am–5pm; July and August, 9am–6pm;
only reserved groups at other times.
Admission charge. On the N874, 3km east
of Bastogne.*

BOUILLON

One of many Ardennes towns with
dramatic locations in steep river valleys,
in this case the River Semois, Bouillon
also boasts one of Belgium's finest
medieval castles.

Château de Bouillon (Bouillon Castle)

Dating from the 12th century, but with
traces from the 10th, the castle is still a
powerful-looking military fortification
overlooking the town; in medieval times
it must have appeared awesome.
Bouillon Castle in the 11th century was

the property of Duke Godefroy de
Bouillon, who led the First Crusade and
was crowned King of Jerusalem.
*Rue des Hautes-Voies 33 (tel: (061)
466257). Open: daily, 1 April to 30 June
and 1 to 30 September, 10am–6pm; 1 July
to 31 August, 9.30am–7pm; March,
October, November and December,
10am–5pm. Admission charge.*

DURBUY

One of the prettiest of Ardennes towns,
situated deep in the valley of the River
Ourthe, in an area of marvellous walking
and cycling country. A 17th-century
château, and viewpoints on the
surrounding cliffs add to the scenic
attractions. Nearby Wéris is notable for
its many Stone Age menhirs, dolmens
and stone circles.
On the N833, 50km south of Liège.

EURO SPACE CENTER

The only one in Europe, based on a space theme park in Texas, Euro Space Center is aimed at both adults and children. As well as exhibits on contemporary and future space operations, such as the Space Shuttle, the Manned Space Station, Lunar and Martian bases, etc, there are weekend and week-long courses for budding astronauts and space enthusiasts from children to corporate executives.
Rue Devant les Hêtres 1, Redu-Transinne (tel: (061) 656465). Open: 16 February to 30 November, daily 10am–5pm. Admission and course charges. Located 1km from exit 24 on the E411.

HAN-SUR-LESSE

The village of Han, on the banks of the River Lesse, is not interesting so much for itself, despite its handsome location, but more for nearby underground caverns and a nature park.

Grottes de Han (Caves of Han)

The most spectacular of the many underground cavern complexes in the Ardennes was discovered by chance in the 19th century and covers some 8sq km, all at the rather chilly temperature of 12°C. The Lesse runs through them, underground for the most part, and in one section there is a lake. A sound-and-light show (*son et lumière*) is part of the guided tour.
Rue Joseph Lamotte 2 (tel: (084) 377212/3). Open: March, November, December, 10am–4pm; April, September, October, 10am–4.30pm; May, June, 9.30am–5pm; July, August, 9.30am–6pm. Closed January and February. Admission charge. Outside Han-sur-Lesse, but access is only by guided tour leaving from the village.

An outing to La Roche-en-Ardenne Castle

Réserve d'Animaux Sauvages (Wild Animal Reserve)

Part of the Lesse and Lomme National Park, a classic riverside Ardennes landscape of 250 hectares which the government has decided to preserve, the Wild Animal Reserve hosts indigenous Ardennes wildlife, such as bison, wild boar, bears, deer, aurochs (a European bison) and wild ponies.
Practical details are identical with those of the Caves of Han.

LA ROCHE-EN-ARDENNE

Of all the dramatically sited Ardennes towns, this must be the best situated. A bend of the River Ourthe sweeps through a plunging valley, and La Roche nestles on the valley floor and hugs the hillsides. An 11th-century castle on the Diester cliff above the town is now no more than a ruin, but a romantic reward for the hike up.

At nearby Nisramont (10km on the N834 and N843) and Nadrin (11km on the N860) there are belvederes which provide superb views over the river and surrounding forests.

A hunting museum is housed inside Lavaux-Sainte-Anne Castle

LAVAUX-SAINTE-ANNE

The Château Féodal (Feudal Castle) of the little village of Lavaux-Sainte-Anne, dating from 1193, would be worth visiting for no other reason than its moated walls with three towers and a keep amid open countryside. Inside, however, is the Musée de la Chasse et de la Conservation de la Nature (Museum of Hunting and Nature Conservation) which adds interest with animal displays (some of them grisly) linking nature and hunting.

Lavaux-Sainte-Anne (tel: (084) 388362). Open: 1 March to 31 October, daily 9am–6pm; 1 November to 28 February, 9am–5pm. Admission charge. Exit 22a on the E411.

REDU

Famed as the 'Village of Books', this charmingly quaint place lives up to its reputation, even if a little self-consciously. Redu has been given over almost entirely to the sale of second-hand books. Arts and crafts boutiques have joined the bookshops, and artisanal food and drink is available to refresh jaded browsers.

Bookshops are open throughout the year, *but weekends are best out of season. Exit 24 on the E411.*

SAINT-HUBERT

The little town of Saint-Hubert is the centre of the Ardennes hunting tradition, and is named after the patron-saint of hunters.

Basilique Saint-Hubert (Saint Hubert's Basilica)

Dating from the 16th century, the mixed Romanesque and Gothic-style church seems doubly imposing.

Place de la Basilique (tel: (061) 612388). Open: daily 9.30am–5pm. Admission free. Town centre.

Musée de la Vie Rurale en Wallonie (Museum of Rural Life in Wallonia)

A classic open-air museum, with 25 typical farmhouses and workshops giving an idea of how people lived and worked in the Walloon countryside in the past.

Fourneau Saint-Michel (tel: (084) 210890). Open: 1 March to mid-November, daily 9am–5pm (6pm in July and August). Admission charge. Located 8km north of Saint-Hubert on the N84.

Spa's thermal Baths Establishment is a source of health

Etablissement des Bains (Baths Establishment)

The neo-classical heart of Spa's water-therapy industry dates from 1868. The baths here are supplied with mineral water from the nearby Hautes Fagnes Nature Park and are a highlight of any visit. Other treatments, such as peat baths, require a medical examination.

Place Royale (tel: (087) 772560). Open: Monday to Friday 8am–noon, 1.30–4pm; Saturday 8am–noon. Charge for treatments.

Lac de Warfaaz

A pleasantly situated small lake outside Spa, with pedal-boats and mountain-bikes for hire, lakeside café terraces and a promenade through the trees along the shore.

Three kilometres north of Spa on the N628.

SPA

This elegant Ardennes town is the source of the English word 'spa' (see pages 126–7). Its health-giving mineral springs have been famous since Roman times and have lured many VIPs, including Russia's Tsar Peter the Great.

Spa Monopole

The bottling plant of the company that exploits the mineral waters. A guided tour includes an explanation of how ultra-pure Spa Reine water originates from snowfall in the nearby Hautes Fagnes Nature Reserve then spends three years filtering through layers of peat and sand before emerging at the spring.

Rue Auguste Laporte (tel: (087) 774311). Open: Monday to Friday 9am–11.30am and 1–3.30pm. Admission free. Adjacent to Spa railway station.

Recalling Peter the Great's visit to Spa in 1717

Pouhon Pierre le Grand (Peter the Great Spring)

A light and airy pavilion built over the source of a metallic-tasting spring, it formerly doubled as a winter garden and now hosts art exhibitions.

Place Pierre le Grand (tel: (087) 772510). Open: Easter to October, daily 10am–noon, 2–5.30pm; November to Easter, 2–5pm and weekends also 10am–noon. Admission free, but nominal charge for the water.

TELECOO

Nestling in a scenic gorge where the River Amblève tumbles over the Cascade de Coo (Coo Waterfall), Telecoo Amusement Park would be notable enough for its location alone. A chair-lift ride to the summit of a nearby hill offers a splendid view along the plunging river valley. Activities include canoeing, fishing, minigolf, mini train, go-karting, motorcycle cross and a racing course.

Coo village (tel: (080) 684265). Open: daily, 1 May to 30 September and on weekends during winter. Admission charge. On the N633 near Stavelot.

BATTLE OF THE BULGE

As Allied armies battled towards Hitler's Germany in late 1944, the Ardennes sector remained quiet. American and German soldiers in this backwater of the war considered themselves lucky, but the calm was shattered on 16 December by a heavy artillery barrage. Out of the misty, snow-covered forests charged the first tanks and assault troops of a massive German offensive.

Some surprised and outnumbered Americans fled or surrendered; others stood their ground. The attackers headed for the River Meuse, and war correspondents, noting their deep penetration of Allied lines, gave the Ardennes Offensive its popular name: the Battle of the Bulge.

Bastogne became the symbol of a battle that cost 80,000 American and 100,000 German casualties. Called on to surrender the surrounded town, General Anthony MacAuliffe delivered a one-word reply: 'Nuts'. Bitter fighting halted the offensive, then American reinforcements slowly pushed the Germans back. By February the battle was over but the Ardennes lay devastated.

A Royal Tiger tank at La Gleize

OSTKANTONE (EAST CANTONS)

The mainly German-speaking East Cantons area is almost alpine in character, except that the mountains are on the small side. It lies along the border with Germany, Holland and Luxembourg. When language and history are added to scenic beauty and Belgium's biggest national park, it seems surprising that this area is not better known abroad.

Once part of Prussia, then Germany, the East Cantons were ceded to Belgium after World War I. Hitler annexed them in 1940; they were liberated in 1944; briefly re-annexed during the Ardennes Offensive of December 1944; and restored to Belgium in 1945. Since then, the residents have claimed to be 'the best Belgians of all'.

BURG-REULAND

A 1,000-year-old village in the valley of the River Our, Burg-Reuland has a notable architectural and historical legacy.

Burg (Castle)

A ruined 11th-century castle on a hill above the village. Originally the site of a Roman fort, the later Frankish royal château once hosted Charlemagne. Now its broken walls are a testimony to centuries of feuding on the frontier. Restoration work is bringing both the look and the history of the castle into sharper focus.

Burgstrasse (tel: (080) 420046). Open: school holiday times only, 10am–5pm. Admission charge. Uphill from the village centre.

Sankt-Stephanus-Kirche (Saint Stephen's Church)

Inside the church is a statue of Saint Lucia wearing a beatific expression despite being transfixed by a sword. Other 'residents' of the 17th-century church are Baron Balthasar von Pallant and his wife Elisabeth, deceased early in that century and immortalised in effigy

Inside Saint Stephen's Church

on their black schist sarcophagus.
Dorfstrasse (tel: (080) 329131). Open: daily. Admission free. Village centre.

BURG-RHEINHARDSTEIN (RHEINHARDSTEIN CASTLE)

A superb, reconstructed medieval castle in a fairy-tale setting above the River Warche, Rheinhardstein was once owned by the Metternich family, one of whose members was the renowned 19th-century statesman of the Habsburg Empire. Having been virtually demolished, the castle was rescued by Belgian Professor Jean Overloop and now stands as an atmospheric reminder of turbulent times in this much-fought-over corner of Europe.
Ovifat (tel: (080) 446440). Guided visits only. Open: mid-June to mid-September, Sunday 2.15pm, 3.15, 4.15pm, 5.15pm; July and August, Tuesday, Thursday and Saturday 3.30pm only. Admission charge. Outside Ovifat village, near Robertville.

EUPEN

With a population of just 17,000, this handsome, bustling little town near Aachen is 'capital' of the East Cantons, location of the local parliament and cultural centre of Belgium's German-speaking community. Eupen's Rosenmontag (Rose Monday) carnival is one of Belgium's most impressive (see page 152).

Exekutive (Parliament)

The cloth industry that gave Eupen its prosperity has left it a legacy of fine patrician houses, one of which, dating from 1761, houses the East Cantons government.
Klötzerbahn 32 (tel: (087) 744075). Guided visits arranged in advance only. Admission free. Town centre.

East Canton's parliament building

Hertogenwald

The dense Hertogenwald forest outside Eupen offers plenty of fresh-air activities, including walks beside forest-lined Eupener Stausee (Eupen Lake) and across the high dam that creates a reservoir containing 25 million cubic metres of drinking water.
From Eupen, the N68 to Malmédy and N67 to Monschau run through the forest. Eupen Lake is a few kilometres east of the town, off the N67.

Sankt-Nikolaus-Pfarrkirche (Saint Nicholas's Church)

The German baroque-style church dating from 1721–6 and its two symmetrical towers with bulbous spires dominates the elegant old town centre.
Marktplatz (tel: (087) 742062). Open: daily. Admission free. Town centre.

EUROPADENKMAL (EUROPE MONUMENT)

Situated beside the River Our at the meeting-point of Belgium, Germany and Luxembourg, this monument in the form of standing stones commemorates the founders of European unity and celebrates the community of interest between European nations.
Drielländereck, Georges-Wagner-Brücke (Georges Wagner Bridge), Ouren. Open: daily. Admission free. Follow the 'Europadenkmal' signs from Ouren.

Lazing along on the water at Bütgenbach Lake

HAUTES FAGNES (HIGH FENS)

This bleak, high moorland plateau includes a nature reserve valued for its rare flora and fauna (see pages 120–1). The Hautes Fagnes are popular with weekend ramblers as well as scientists and ecologists.

A series of wooden walkways crosses the boggy peat moors, offering the only viable way of penetrating a mysterious landscape created by the receding glaciers of the last Ice Age. The landscape is fragile and access may be restricted for its protection.

There are entrances to the Nature Reserve at Baraque-Michel and Mont-Rigi. The latter has a special area, the Fagne de la Poleûr, with a walkway which has been marked out as an educational tour. It offers a not-too-strenuous introduction to the Hautes Fagnes while saving other areas from damaging human interference.

Between Eupen and Robertville. The reserve closes at times of fire hazard and during critical wildlife breeding periods. Access times and regulations available from Botrange Nature Centre. Free. N68 and N676.

Centre Nature à Botrange (Botrange Nature Centre)

Headquarters of the Hautes Fagnes Nature Park which covers much of the East Cantons. A visitor centre features exhibitions, documentation, audio-visual presentations, bicycle-hire (cross-country skis in winter). Guided tours of the nature reserve leave from here.

The nearby Signal de Botrange is a tower that marks the highest point in Belgium, 694m above sea level.
Botrange (tel: (080) 445781). Open: Tuesday to Sunday 10am–6pm, Monday 1–6pm (closed for 2 weeks in November). Admission charge. N676 between Mont-Rigi and Sourbrodt.

LAC DE ROBERTVILLE (ROBERTVILLE LAKE)

One of several 'great lakes' in the East Cantons, Robertville's beaches and boating facilities are popular.
The lake lies south of Robertville village.

SANKT-VITH

An old market town, Sankt-Vith was all but destroyed during the Ardennes Offensive of 1944, which accounts for its pristinely modern look. However, its rebuilders avoided the dubious charms of modern architecture and retained the spirit of the original town.
Exit 15 on the E42.

MALMÉDY

A mainly French-speaking commune in the mainly German-speaking East Cantons, this market and commercial town is situated where the River Amblève valley is overlooked by the Hautes Fagnes plateau. Malmédy is famed for its pre-Lenten carnival (see page 153).
Exit 11 on the E42.

Carnival capers in Malmédy

STAUSEE BÜTGENBACH (BUTGENBACH LAKE)

This lake is one of the more overtly touristic areas in the East Cantons, and includes the Sportzentrum Worriken (Worriken Sports Centre), notable for its Swiss-style chalets and water sports.
The lake lies east of Bütgenbach village.

VENNBAHN RAILWAY

Originally built during the East Cantons' Prussian era in the 1880s, the Vennbahn runs on a winding route between Eupen and Büllingen, but now only operates a tourist train on certain days between April and October.
Vennbahn Raeren, 4730 Raeren (tel: (087) 852487). Timetable is variable and reservations are needed.

OVER THE BORDER

The East Cantons are a frontier zone, and some of the area's charm lies just across the border in Germany, Holland and Luxembourg.

Germany
The almost fairy-tale town of Monschau, and Charlemagne's capital Aachen, are both near Eupen; the Schnee Eifel mountain, part of the trans-border Hautes Fagnes–North Eifel Nature Park, is near Schönberg.

Holland
The casino at Valkenburg and the *kastelen* (castles) of Limburg are within easy reach.

Luxembourg
The charming town of Clervaux occupies the floor of a deep gorge south of Burg-Reuland.

HAINAUT

Called the 'green province', Hainaut is also Belgium's southernmost province, a land of rolling countryside adjoining France. Its main city is industrial Charleroi, although there is also historic Tournai (see pages 116–17) and Mons.

Hainaut has long been an important agricultural area. During the Industrial Revolution and up to recent times, however, it was also a centre of coal and heavy industry.

CANAL DU CENTRE (CENTRAL CANAL)

At La Louvière, several attractions are combined to give an idea of life on the inland waterways (see pages 132–3). Horse-drawn barges and conventional tour boats make excursions, and there are hydraulic boat-lifts and the Musée Flottant de la Navigation en Wallonie (Walloon Museum of Inland Navigation).

Information is available from Cantine des Italiens, Rue Tout-y-Faut, La Louvière (tel: (064) 662561). Open: 1 May to 30 September, various times. Admission and excursion charges. Exit 20 from the E42.

CHEMIN DE FER A VAPEUR DES 3 VALLÉES (3 VALLEYS STEAM TRAIN)

The steam trains based at Mariembourg re-create a piece of railway history between several towns and villages in the scenic area called the Botte du Hainaut (Hainaut's Boot).

Station de Mariembourg (tel: (060) 311078). Open: 1 April to 30 September. Excursion charge. Located 12km south of Philippeville on the N5.

CHIMAY

A village in the extreme south, known

for the nearby, imposing Abbaye Nôtre-Dame-de-Scourmont, whose monks brew the Trappist Chimay beer.
Only the courtyard is open to the public. Located 10km south of Chimay.

DOMAINE DE BELOEIL (BELOEIL ESTATE)

The estate of the Prince of Ligne includes one of Belgium's noblest castles, the 17th-century Château de Beloeil. Its lavish interior includes tapestries, paintings, and mannekins re-creating an 18th-century scene. The grounds are superb, with parks and a lake. There is also Minibel, with miniatures of well-known Belgian buildings.

Rue du Château 11, Beloeil (tel: (069) 689426). Open: 1 April to 1 November, daily 10am–6pm. Admission charge. Beloeil village centre.

GRAND-HORNU

A monument to Belgium's industrialisation and to a paternalistic employer, Grand-Hornu is a remarkable piece of industrial archaeology. Seeming more like the ruins of an aristocrat's country villa than the coal-mining works that it was, Grand-Hornu was founded by Henri de Gorge in 1825 as a model, integrated working and living environment.

Rue Sainte-Louise 82, Hornu (tel: (065) 770712). Open: 1 March to 30 September, Tuesday to Friday 10am–noon and 2–6pm; 1 October to 28 February, Tuesday to Friday 10am–noon and 2–4pm, closed Monday. Admission charge. Exit 25 from E19, west of Mons.

MAISON VAN GOGH (VAN GOGH HOUSE)

The Dutch artist lived for a time in the

A museum devoted to canals and canal barges lines the banks of the Central Canal

then desperately poor area south of Mons called the Borinage.
Rue du Pavillon 3, Cuesmes (tel: (065) 355611). Open: Tuesday to Sunday 10am–6pm. Admission charge. Exit 2 from R5 (Mons ring road).

MUSÉE INTERNATIONAL DU CARNAVAL ET DU MASQUE (INTERNATIONAL MUSEUM OF CARNIVAL AND MASKS)

Located in Binche, where Belgium's most astonishing carnival erupts in the streets during February (see page 153), this colourful museum celebrates carnival traditions and costumes from all over the world.
Rue Saint-Moustier 10, Binche (tel: (064) 335741). Open: 2 November to 31 March,

Monday to Friday 9am–noon and 1–5pm, weekends 2–6pm; 1 April to 31 October, Monday to Friday 9am–noon and 2–6pm, Saturday 2–6pm, Sunday 10am–noon and 2–6pm. Admission charge. Near the Grand-Place.

RONQUIÈRES

'Ships in the air' are the unusual attraction at the Ronquières boat-lift, where canal barges and pleasure boats are carried in huge tanks on a 1.4km-long elevator track, which raises or lowers them by up to 68m.
Plan Incliné de Ronquières (tel: (065) 360464). Open: 1 May to 31 August, daily 10am–6pm. Admission charge. Located 5km south of Ronquières on the N534.

LIÈGE

Liège is a city of saints and sinners. The saints adorn a vast number of churches whose grandeur reflects that of the city's historic rulers, the Prince-Bishops. They might, however, be indulgent towards sinners whose main 'vice' is over-enthusiastic patronage of cafés and restaurants – Liège is one of Belgium's most hot-blooded cities.

Washed by the River Meuse, it has both scenic riverside walks and industrial eyesores. The Prince-Bishops, who ruled from 980 to 1794, gave it a monumental look appropriate to an ecclesiastical capital, but the city's finest building no longer exists. French troops set fire to the medieval Cathédrale Saint-Lambert (Saint Lambert's Cathedral) in 1794.

Twin towers of Saint Barthélemy's Church in Liège

AQUARIUM

Liège has a superb Aquarium, equipped with 40 tanks in which different marine and aquatic environments have been recreated.
Institut de Zoologie, Quai Van Beneden 22 (tel: (041) 665000). Open: Monday to Friday 10am–12.30pm and 1.30–5.pm, weekends 10.30am–12.30pm and 2–6pm. Admission charge. Riverside.

LA BATTE

Liège's weekend market (see page 145).

CATHÉDRALE SAINT-PAUL (SAINT PAUL'S CATHEDRAL)

Liège's Gothic cathedral is impressive, but only a shadow of the destroyed Saint Lambert's Cathedral. Its rich Trésor (Treasury) has a superb Réliquaire de Charles le Téméraire (Reliquary of Charles the Bold) in gold and silver. Charles, Duke of Burgundy, earns his sobriquet in this case because his face is identical to Saint George's.
Rue Bonne-Fortune 6 (tel: (041) 220426). Open: daily 10am–5pm. Admission charge. City centre south.

CHARLEMAGNE (CHARLES THE GREAT)

An equestrian statue of the King of the Franks, born in Liège, and crowned Holy Roman Emperor in AD800, keeps a close eye on his former dominions.
Between Boulevard Piercot and Boulevard d'Avroy, outside Parc d'Avroy (Avroy Park).

EGLISE SAINT-BARTHÉLEMY (SAINT BARTHÉLEMY'S CHURCH)

A Romanesque church noted for its Font Baptismaux (Baptismal Font), which has been called one of the 'seven wonders of Belgium'. Created by Renier de Huy between 1107 and 1118, this bronze masterpiece of Mosan art has a base surrounded by 10 weighed-down oxen and baptismal scenes (including the Baptism of Christ) carved on its sides.
Place Saint-Barthélemy (tel: (041) 234998). Open: Monday to Saturday 10am–noon and 2–5pm; Sunday 2–5pm. Admission free. Between En Hors-Château and En Féronstrée.

MONTAGNE DE BUEREN (BUEREN HILL)

The 374 steps of this steep passageway leading to the centuries-old hilltop Citadel are an impressive (and tiring) reminder of the topography that contributed to Liège's historic role as a fortified city. The Citadel retains no more than vestiges of its former military works, and at its heart stands a modern hospital, but the view from its ramparts is evidence that the position controlled the surrounding territory.

Begins 250m from Prince-Bishop's Palace, off En Hors-Château.

MUSÉE CURTIUS (CURTIUS MUSEUM)

The mansion of 17th-century arms dealer Jean Curtius now houses a museum of local archaeology and fine arts. A separate section forms the Musée

Coming down is about as hard as going up the Bueren Hill's 374 steps

du Verre (Glass Museum), with around 9,000 beautiful works of glass and porcelain.

Quai de Maestricht 13 (tel: (041) 219404). Open: Monday, Thursday and Saturday 2–5pm, Wednesday, Friday and 2nd and 4th Sunday of the month 10am–1pm. Admission charge. Riverside.

MUSÉE D'ARMES (WEAPONS MUSEUM)

Liège is, and has been for centuries, an important centre for weapons manufacture. Among the museum's 12,500 exhibits are sidearms, rifles and muskets.

Quai de Maestricht 8 (tel: (041) 219400). Open: Monday, Thursday, Saturday and 1st and 3rd Sunday of the month 10am–1pm; Wednesday and Friday 2–5pm; closed Tuesday. Admission charge. Riverfront.

TCHANTCHÈS

The city's own marionette 'cheekie chappie', Tchantchès's stamping-ground is the 'République Libre d'Outremeuse' ('Free Republic of Outremeuse'), the working-class district across the river and a spirited and independent-minded entity, just like Tchantchès himself. The marionette even engages in puppet-combat with the Emperor Charlemagne. He has a monument and a museum dedicated to him, and a collection of costumes donated by his admirers.

Musée Tchantchès, Rue Surlet 56 (tel: (041) 427575). Open: Tuesday and Thursday 2–4pm (closed July). Admission charge. Outremeuse.

MUSÉE D'ART RELIGIEUX ET D'ART MOSAN (MUSEUM OF RELIGIOUS AND MOSAN ART)

Some of the finest works of local religious craftsmanship are displayed in this museum. Paintings and sculptures are in abundance, as well as superbly ornate gold and silver vessels – monstrances, chalices and reliquaries – studded with precious stones and pearls.
Rue Mère-Dieu 1 (tel: (041) 214225).
Open: Tuesday to Saturday 1–6pm;
Sunday 11am–4pm. Closed Monday.
Admission charge. Located behind the
Prince-Bishops' Palace, off En Hors-
Château.

Le Perron fountain, a popular symbol of the city's history

MUSÉE DE LA VIE WALLONNE (MUSEUM OF WALLOON LIFE)

An old Franciscan convent makes an atmospheric location for showing Walloon culture and tradition. The museum displays everything from farm life and porcelain-manufacture to local cuisine and the Walloon art of marionettes (puppet theatre). Of the latter, there are some beautifully made marionettes from the romantic tale of Charlemagne, his son Roland, and the flight of the four Aymon brothers from Charlemagne's wrath on the horse Bayard.
Cour des Mineurs (tel: (041) 236094).
Open: Tuesday to Saturday 10am–5pm,
Sunday 10am–4pm. Closed Monday.
Admission charge. Located 100m from the
Prince-Bishops' Palace, off En Hors-
Château.

PALAIS DES PRINCE-EVEQUES (PALACE OF THE PRINCE-BISHOPS)

Victor Hugo said he had never before seen such a 'strange, bizarre and marvellous' building. Begun in the 9th century, the vast palace was rebuilt in the 16th and is said to be the world's biggest secular Gothic structure. Its courtyard, with porticoes supported by 60 decorated columns, and a second, inner courtyard with gardens and an ornamental pool, may be visited.
Place Saint-Lambert, in the heart of the city.

LE PERRON

An ornately decorated fountain, topped by a sculpture of the Three Graces, that is a symbol of the city's history.
Place du Marché, between the Prince-Bishops' Palace and the Hôtel de Ville (Town Hall).

SART TILMAN

The out-of-town campus of the Université de Liège (Liège University) is a wooded, green domain. In addition to the modern architecture of the buildings, the campus is an open-air sculpture park, dotted with intriguingly modern works. The 17th-century Château de Colonstère (Colonstère Castle) adds a counterpoint to all this modernity, and the whole area is popular for weekend walks.
Route de Condroz (tel: (041) 665301).
Open: permanently. Admission free.
Located 2km south of Liège, on the N63.

VAL-SAINT-LAMBERT

Beauty is the attraction here, in a dingy, hot and smoky, and somewhat broken-down factory where some of the world's finest handmade and engraved crystal is produced (see page 136). The complex includes an exhibition room, a gift shop and a workshop with seats where visitors can see glass being blown and carved direct from the furnace by the company's craftsmen.
Rue du Val 245, Seraing (tel: (041) 370960). Open: daily 9am–5pm. Admission charge for workshop.

The richly ornamented baptismal font from Saint Barthélemy's Church (see page 106)

Seraing is 5km southwest of Liège on the N90.

For further information on Liège, contact: Office du Tourisme, En Féronstrée 92, B-4000 Liège (tel: (041) 219221 or 222456).

THE SIMENON CASE

Liège-born author Georges Simenon died in 1989 at the age of 86, by which time no fewer than 84 of the famous Inspector Maigret detective novels had emerged from his typewriter, along with another hundred or so books. Born in the Outremeuse, the working-class district of Liège, Simenon loved the sights and sounds and feel of this poor but spirited quarter, and they permeate many of his books: he said that whatever a writer experienced in his first 17 years would remain with him for life.

Simenon left his manuscripts and other material to the Fonds Simenon (Simenon Foundation) at Liège University. The city has named a street after him and the tourist office has a walking tour of the Outremeuse, where Maigret 'learned' the lessons he would one day put to good use on the streets of Paris.

MEUSE VALLEY

The River Meuse, on its L-shaped course through Belgium, is Wallonia's geographical dividing line, separating the rugged Ardennes hills from the gently rolling plains to the west. Its often sheer valley and pleasant resort towns make it a popular tourist destination (see pages 106–9, 112–13 and 120–1).

ABBAYE DE MAREDSOUS (MAREDSOUS ABBEY)

Situated in the steeply forested valley of the Molignée, a stream that runs into the Meuse, the neo-Gothic Benedictine abbey opened in 1872. Famed for its beer and cheese as well as its historical religious research, the abbey is popular with visitors, who come to experience its calm atmosphere and artisanal products.
Denée (tel: (082) 698211). Open: daily 9am–6pm. Admission free (except for an interior exposition room). Located 4km from the N932, outside Denée.

CHÂTEAU D'ANNEVOIE (ANNEVOIE CASTLE)

The 18th-century château's fountains and gardens are a memorable sight, thanks to their pastoral setting above the River Meuse. Crystal-clear water from the fast-flowing Annevoie stream powers the fountains. Their shapes, together with the gardens' floral displays, trees and pools, and the estate's imposing castle create a splendid visual feast.
Annevoie-Rouillon (tel: (082) 611555). Open: end of March to beginning November, daily 9.30am–6.30pm. Admission charge. Located 2km along the N932 from the Namur–Dinant road.

CHÂTEAU DE FREYR (FREYR CASTLE)

The 16th-century château and its ornamental gardens occupy a place of great beauty beside the river.
Domaine de Freyr (tel: (082) 222200). Open: 1 July to 31 August, weekends and public holidays only 2–6pm. Admission charge. N96, 6km south of Dinant.

CHÂTEAU DE VÊVES (VÊVES CASTLE)

A perfect example of a romantic medieval castle, Vêves's pointed towers and granite walls loom high over an outlook of forests and steep valleys. The same family has owned the castle for centuries, and as well as guided tours they host weddings and other receptions.
Noisy 2, Celles-sur-Lesse (tel: (082) 666395). Open: 1 April to 31 October, 10am–noon and 1.30–6pm, closed Monday. Admission charge. Off the N910, 2km south of Celles.

DINANT

One of the Meuse Valley's most handsome resort towns, Dinant is also a historic centre with a rich artisitic and cultural tradition.

Citadelle (Citadel)

A citadel was as important as a cathedral to River Meuse towns, and Dinant's follows the traditional pattern. Sited high on a dominant cliff, it was begun in 1051 and variously expanded and destroyed through the centuries. Among its cavernous galleries is a Musée d'Armes (Weapons Museum).
Le Prieuré 25 (accessible by cable-car) (tel: (082) 222119/223670). Open: 1 April to 30 September, daily 10am–6pm; 1 October to 31 March, daily 10am–4pm, except Friday between 1 November and 28 February (closed). Admission and cable-car charge. Overlooks the town on the right bank of the river.

Looking across the River Meuse towards Dinant Citadel and the Collégiale Nôtre-Dame

Collégiale Nôtre-Dame (Church of Our Lady)

The distinctive riverside church, with a bulbous spire dating from 1697, has become a symbol of Dinant. Like the town, it has been rebuilt several times, most recently after each of the world wars.

Place Astrid (tel: (082) 222707). Open: daily. Admission free. On the riverfront beside the road bridge.

HUY

A small but historic River Meuse resort, midway between Liège and Namur. Equipped with a cliff-top Citadelle (Citadel); a richly decorated church, the Collégiale Nôtre-Dame (Church of Our Lady); and an elegant Grand-Place (Main Square) with an 18th-century Hôtel de Ville (Town Hall), Huy has all the ingredients of an important riverside town.

Musée Communal (Community Museum)

Housed in a 17th-century Franciscan priory, the museum features aspects of history, folklore and life in the Meuse Valley. Among its collection is the Beau Dieu de Huy (Beautiful God of Huy), a masterly 13th-century sculpture depicting Christ.

Rue Vankeerberghen (tel: (085) 232435). Open: 1 April to 31 October, daily 2–6pm.

NAMUR

When Belgium 'reorganised' itself into regions, the French-speakers chose Namur as capital of Wallonia. A curious choice from an international perspective – Liège, Charleroi and Tournai are better known abroad – this resort town of 40,000 inhabitants at the confluence of the River Meuse and River Sambre is certainly an attractive location for a capital.

Namur is dominated by its 2,000-year-old Citadel which, far from protecting the citizens, proved an irresistible lure to invaders. Yet an often tragic history has left few visible scars on the town, and no visit to Belgium would be complete without a look at this 'other' capital.

The light Italianate style of Namur's Saint Aubin's Cathedral

CASINO

One of Namur's more wordly attractions, the riverside casino dates from 1911 and is one reason why the town is so popular with visitors – those who win, at any rate.

Casino de Namur, Avenue Baron de Moreau (tel: (081) 220334).

CATHÉDRAL SAINT-AUBIN (SAINT AUBIN'S CATHEDRAL)

A domed structure dating from 1751, whose bright interior and Italianate style, quite different from most Belgian churches, is accounted for by its Italian architect, Pizzoni. The cupola is decorated with bas-reliefs and the whole ensemble has an almost ethereal feel, complemented by paintings by the Rubens School and Van Dyck, and an ornate marble interior.

Place Saint-Aubin (tel: (081) 221333). Open: daily. Admission free.

Musée Diocésain (Diocesan Museum)

Incorporates the Trésor (Treasury) of the Cathédral Saint-Aubin, a small but impressive collection of art works, vestments, sculptures, reliquaries and other religious artefacts.

Place du Chapitre 1 (tel: (081) 222164). Open: Easter Tuesday to 31 October, Tuesday to Saturday 10am–noon and 2.30–6pm, Sunday 2.30–6pm. Admission charge. Adjacent to the cathedral.

CITADELLE (CITADEL)

Two scenic drives, the Route Merveilleuse and the Route des Panoramas, wind up the steep cliffside to the Citadel, whose defensive installations sprawl across the summit. An alternative ascent, which gives an even better view over the town, the

Meuse Valley and the Ardennes forests, is by *téléférique* (cable-car) from Place Pied-du-Château.

The Citadel has been transformed from its age-old military role (it began as a Celtic hill fort, then the Romans established a fort there) to the more peaceable pursuits of a tourist centre. Its 15th- to 19th-century defences, barracks and storage depots are now occupied by restaurants, shops and even a local perfume-maker, Parfumerie Guy Delforge.

Centre Attractif Reine Fabiola (Queen Fabiola Attractions Centre)

A children's playground near the top of the Citadel.
Chaussée Berenger (tel: (081) 738413).
Open: 1 April to 31 October, daily during school holidays, Wednesday and weekends only at other times, 11am–6pm. Admission charge.

Château de Namur (Château of Namur)

The impressive 19th-century château, now a hotel, takes pride of place at the Citadel's summit, and is surrounded by fine gardens with an ornamental fish-pond, beside which newly-weds like to be photographed.
Avenue de l'Ermitage 1 (tel: (081) 742630).

Musée de la Forêt (Museum of the Forest)

Focuses on the Ardennes forests and streams, with glass cases and vast dioramas featuring the problems of conservation and deforestation as. well as the lives of the animals, birds, fishes, trees and plants that are the main reason why the Ardennes are so popular.

Café terraces and fountain in the old centre of Namur

Route Merveilleuse 9 (tel: (081) 743894).
Open: 1 April to 31 October, Saturday to Thursday 9am–noon and 2–5pm. Closed Friday. Admission charge.

LE CORBEIL

This is the old quarter of Namur, squeezed into the angle where the River Sambre meets the River Meuse. Although not especially notable for imposing architecture – but look for the Beffroi (Belfry) in Place d'Armes – Le Corbeil's narrow alleyways are an atmospheric location for strolling and shopping. In good weather, restaurants and cafés spread their tables on to the cobbles and the Saturday market in the Marché-aux-Légumes adds its own spice of life to the mixture.

The River Meuse seen from the vantage point of Namur Citadel

MUSÉE ARCHÉOLOGIQUE (ARCHAEOLOGICAL MUSEUM)

Housed in the 15th-century Renaissance-style butchers' market beside the River Sambre, the museum displays important remains of the Roman Empire along the Meuse Valley. The region was particularly noted for wealthy country villas and the finds reflect everyday life, and death, in isolated agricultural communities.
Rue du Pont (tel: (081) 231631). Open: Tuesday to Friday 10am–5pm, weekends 10.30am–5pm. Admission charge.

MUSÉE DE GROESBEECK DE CROIX (GROESBEECK DE CROIX MUSEUM)

The elegant lifestyle of a wealthy 18th-century Namurois family is illustrated by way of a brilliant display of the decorative arts in this well-tended bourgeois town house.
Rue Joseph Saintraint 5 (tel: (081) 222139). Open: Tuesday to Sunday for

visits on the hour only, 10am–noon and 2–5pm. Admission charge.

MUSÉE DES ARTS ANCIENS NAMUROIS (MUSEUM OF CLASSIC NAMUR ARTS)

Despite its all-embracing name, the museum focuses on religious art from the Meuse Valley, of which it has a fine medieval collection.
Rue de Fer 24 (tel: (081) 220065). Open: Tuesday to Sunday 10am–6pm (5pm 1 November to 1 April). Admission charge.

MUSÉE FÉLICIEN ROPS (FELICIEN ROPS MUSEUM)

Namur seems to have mixed feelings about its wayward 19th-century painter, whose artistic bent lay towards the bizarre and erotic, and who delighted in shocking the bourgeois respectability of his age.

The Félicien Rops Museum is tucked away down a side-street, but his works are given all the exposure he could have desired.

Rue Fumal 12, 5000 Namur (tel: (081) 220110). Open: daily 10am–5pm (6pm in summer); closed Monday except during July and August. Admission charge.

PARC LOUISE-MARIE (MARIE LOUISE PARK)

A pretty little park beside the River Sambre, with a duck-pond, grottoes and gardens, that makes for a peaceful stroll with small children.

Located between Rue de Bruxelles and Boulevard Frère-Orban. Open: daily. Admission free.

RIVERS SAMBRE AND MEUSE

Boats leave from Namur on trips along both rivers. An interesting modern sculpture beside the Meuse shows the four Aymon brothers in flight from the Holy Roman Emperor Charlemagne on the horse Bayard, which seems set to leap across the wide river.

Boat trips: Avenue Baron Huart (tel: (082) 222315).

WÉPION

This riverside village just outside Namur is the centre of Belgium's strawberry-growing district and is the country's self-appointed 'Strawberry Capital'. Wépion has the Musée de la Fraise (Strawberry Museum) devoted to this summer delicacy.

Musée de la Fraise, Chaussée de Dinant 137, Wépion (tel: (081) 460113). Open: 15 April to 15 September, daily 3–6pm, closed Monday. Admission charge.

THE ROMANS IN BELGIUM

Belgium first appeared on history's stage amid a welter of violence and blood, courtesy of those hard-fisted conquerors, the Romans. Julius Caesar's legions had a hard time of it during the 50s BC, however, and by his own account the Belgae were the bravest fighters he ever faced.

After a rebellion under Ambiorix, which was savagely suppressed, the Belgae's lands became the Roman province of Gallia Belgica. The frontier of the empire moved to the Rhine and Belgium became an agricultural backwater, dotted with villas, and administered from two towns, present-day Tongeren and Tournai.

Some of today's Belgian attractions have been celebrated since Roman times, the mineral waters of Spa, for example (see pages 98 and 126–7). Pliny the Elder, in his *Natural History,* wrote of 'a remarkable spring that emerges in several places and tastes of iron', located in the Ardennes area, and whose waters 'purge the body and cure fevers'.

Early in the 5th century, Germanic tribes erupted across the Rhine, tearing the Western Empire apart, and the Franks took their share of the spoils in Belgium and France.

Caesar did not have everything his own way in Belgium

For further information on Namur, contact: Office du Tourisme, Square Léopold, B-5000 Namur (tel: (081) 222859).

Stained glass reflects coloured light throughout Tournai's magnificent Cathedral of Our Lady

TOURNAI (DOORNIK)

Tournai is one of Belgium's oldest cities. For some time after the collapse of Roman power, it was a kind of early European Union capital as the seat of Childéric and Clovis, rulers of the wide-ranging Empire of the Franks.

Today, it is a tranquil small city on the River Escaut/River Schelde (Scheldt), proud of its history and marked with the artistic and architectural signature of its medieval role as an important ecclesiastical centre.

BEFFROI (BELFRY)

With 256 steps leading to its 72m high summit, the 12th-century bell-tower provides a superb view of the town and surrounding countryside. A 43-bell carillon sounds the hours and is also used for concerts.

Grand-Place (tel: (069) 222045). Open: Wednesday to Monday 10am–noon and 2–5.30pm. Admission charge. Adjacent to the Cathedral of Our Lady.

CATHÉDRALE NOTRE-DAME (CATHEDRAL OF OUR LADY)

Tournai's cathedral is a masterpiece of medieval architecture. A harmonious mix of Romanesque and Gothic, begun in the 12th century, it is colossal, with no less than five towers. Its stained-glass windows, featuring religious images and scenes from everyday life, fill the interior with coloured light. Some sculptures and bas-reliefs have been badly damaged, relics of the religious conflicts that plagued the Low Countries.

The Trésor (Treasury) displays outstanding works of medieval craftsmanship, such as the Châsse de Nôtre-Dame (Reliquary of our Lady), a magnificent relic chest in gold and silver, dating from 1205, and featuring eloquently sculpted scenes from the life of Christ.

Place de l'Evêché (tel: (069) 222045). Open: (cathedral) daily 10am–noon and 2–5pm, (treasury) daily 10.15–11.45am and 2.15–4.45pm. Admission: cathedral, free; treasury, charge. Adjacent to the Grand-Place.

GRAND-PLACE (MAIN SQUARE)

The Grand-Place was destroyed during World War II, and the triangular 'square' is a post-war reconstruction. Points of interest are the Halle de Draps (Cloth Hall), whose gilded façade is original but whose interior has been totally rebuilt; and the Église Saint-Quentin (Saint Quentin's Church), whose façade dates from the 13th century, although the interior is modern.

MUSÉE DES BEAUX-ARTS (FINE ARTS MUSEUM)

Housed in a 1928, star-shaped gallery designed by Victor Horta (see page 33), the light and airy museum features many impressive works. Most notable, perhaps, is the *Virgin and Child* by Roger de la Pasture (Rogier van der Weyden), the Flemish 'Primitive' who was born in Tournai. Among many others, there are works by Rubens, Jordaens and Brueghel the Elder.

Enclos Saint-Martin (tel: (069) 222045). Open: Wednesday to Monday 10am–noon and 2–5.30pm. Admission free. Adjacent to the inner ring road.

MUSÉE DU FOLKLORE (FOLKLORE MUSEUM)

Housed in the 17th-century Maison Tournaisienne, the Folklore Museum features a vast collection of objects and scenes from Tournai's past. The top floor has a model of the city in the 16th century.

Réduit des Sions 36 (tel: (069) 222045). Open: Wednesday to Monday 10am–noon and 2–5.30pm. Admission free. In a narrow alley leading off the Grand-Place.

Inside the Fine Arts Museum

MUSÉE DE LA TAPISSERIE (TAPESTRY MUSEUM)

In its restored patrician house from 1825, the museum recalls a little of Tournai's long history of tapestry-making, but focuses more on modern works.

Place Reine Astrid 9 (tel: (069) 222045). Open: Wednesday to Monday 10am–noon and 2–5.30pm. Admission free. Located 200m south of the Grand-Place.

TOUR HENRY VIII (HENRY VIII TOWER)

This gloomy fortification is a reminder that Tournai was once captured by the English in 1513 and held for five years. It incorporates a Musée d'Armes (Weapons Museum), featuring 1,000 years of weaponry and displaying souvenirs of Belgium's World War II Resistance.

Rue de Rempart (tel: (069) 222045). Open: Wednesday to Monday 10am–noon and 2–5.30pm. Admission free. Located 300m from the railway station.

For further information on Tournai, contact: Office du Tourisme, Vieux Marché-aux-Poteries 14, B–7500 Tournai (tel: (069) 222045).

TAPESTRY

The Renaissance biographer Giorgio Vasari, in his *Lives of the Artists* in 1500, wrote of Raphael designing tapestries of gold and silver for Pope Leo X. They were to be produced in Flanders. 'The completed work is of such wonderful beauty', said Vasari, 'that it astonishes anyone who sees it that it could have been possible to weave the hair and beards so finely. The tapestries seem to have been created by a miracle rather than by human skill.'

That miracle was commonplace in Belgian weaving centres like Tournai, Mechelen, Brussels and Oudenaarde. Emperors, kings, lords and bishops all had their tapestries made in Flanders and the results grace museums, royal residences and stately homes throughout Europe. Few alas, remain in Belgium, and even less remains of a trade that dominated artistic fashion from the 15th to the 18th century.

Tapestry-making declined from 50,000 weavers in Flanders during its heyday to today's handful, working at the Royal Tapestry Manufacturers in Mechelen (see page

51) and government restoration agencies as well as some independent artists. Increasing costs, changing fashion and Flemish weavers leaving to work for the competition in other countries combined to undermine Flanders' once pre-eminent position.

Tapestries were hugely expensive, the product of time and painstaking skill,

SI TV · PRETENS A HONNEVR PARVENIR ES DEVX RECOR DEE

Belgian tapestry: 'Works of wonderful beauty'

Left and above: weaving magic with coloured threads at the Royal Tapestry Manufacturer in Mechelen

plus the use of gold and silver thread in addition to the more usual wool and silk. Those made in Brussels during the 16th century for the Spanish Crown, for example, are dazzlingly opulent creations depicting scenes from classical history and from the Bible, with delicately woven golden threads that seem like a fairy-tale come true.

As well as at the Mechelen workshop, tapestries can be seen in Tournai's Tapestry Museum (see page 117), Brussels Town Hall (see page 30) and town halls and museums across the land.

Hautes Fagnes Nature Reserve

Part drive and part walking tour, this fresh-air itinerary traverses the unique Hautes Fagnes Nature Reserve. The Hautes Fagnes owe their origins to the receding glaciers of the last Ice Age. Boggy and tundra-like, wild and lonely, they were once all but inaccessible to man.

Today, however, what remains after centuries of reclamation, peat-gathering and afforestation must be protected if it is to survive. But this can still be a hard environment in bad weather; both its beauties and its dangers should be respected. *Ideally allow a whole day for the tour.*

Begin at Eupen and take the N68 through the Hertogenwald forest, past Baraque-Michel and Mont-Rigi.

EUPEN

This handsome little town is capital of Belgium's small German-speaking community in the East Cantons. Eupen lies only a few kilometres from the Liège–Aachen motorway and offers quick access to the Hautes Fagnes. *Follow the N68 out of Eupen, direction Malmédy.*

HERTOGENWALD

Like the Hautes Fagnes, the Hertogenwald forest is a remnant of a once dominant landscape. Although it spreads across the borders of Belgium, Holland and Germany, the Hertogenwald forest has been trimmed and tamed, but it is still a scenic drive, especially in autumn when the leaves are a dazzling gold. There are also numerous walking trails through the forest. *Continue on the N68 to Baraque-Michel.*

BARAQUE-MICHEL

In a part of the country that often seems deserted, the few stopping points on the road across the Hautes Fagnes, such as Baraque-Michel, can be surprisingly busy. There is a car park, restaurant and *friterie* (chips stall) here, which together account for some of the crowd, but mostly the

A registered guide surveys his domain in Belgium's premier national park

people are walkers taking this main entrance to the nature reserve.

On either side of the road, wooden walkways lead deep into the morass, ensuring a relatively dry-shod crossing even in wet weather. It is mandatory (in addition to being common sense) to stay on the walkways. Various walks are marked on signposts, with round-trips taking anything from one to four or more hours. The further in you go, the more impressive seem the isolation and the sense of nature working through its own agenda.

An interesting spot at Baraque-Michel is the Fischbach-Kapelle, a tiny church built in 1830, where a lantern used to be placed nightly in the window to guide travellers lost in the trackless Hautes Fagnes.
Continue on the N68 to Mont-Rigi.

MONT-RIGI

Another small cluster of human warmth, Mont-Rigi includes a car park, restaurant and a scientific research station operated by the University of Liège. Behind this complex lies the Fagne de la Poleûr, a piece of the moorland which fulfils a double purpose: it has been specially

equipped as a 'didactic' or educational tour of typical Hautes Fagnes ecology; and its relatively easy one- and two-hour round trips make it attractive to casual walkers while sparing more critical and rare habitats from too much human interference.
Just beyond Mont-Rigi is a road junction, where you turn left on to the N676, direction Robertville.

SIGNAL DE BOTRANGE

This tower marks the highest point in Belgium, 694m above sea level.

BOTRANGE

Just off the main road is the Botrange Nature Centre, the administrative headquarters and visitor centre for the whole Hautes Fagnes Nature Park, of which the protected nature reserve is just a small part. In addition to a bookshop, documentation centre and exhibition area, there are cross-country (not mountain) bikes for hire and, in winter, cross-country skis.
Continue on the N676 to Robertville, leaving the Hautes Fagnes behind. From there, signs for Malmédy and the E421 indicate the road to Brussels and Antwerp.

Along the River Meuse

This drive follows a scenic, cliff-lined stretch of the River Meuse from Namur, capital of Wallonia, to the resort town of Dinant. *Allow at least half a day.*

Begin at Namur and head south, mostly on the left-bank N92, although there are occasions to cross by bridge to the right bank. Leave the car as often as possible for a walk along the tow-path.

1 NAMUR

You can drive up Route Merveilleuse or go by cable-car to the Citadelle (Citadel; see page 112), for a superb view over the city and its two rivers, the Sambre and Meuse. In compensation for all the grief this hilltop fortress has brought Namur during the last 1,000 years, it now has an attractive park, and tours by miniature train of its tunnels and defensive works. Below, beside the Meuse, a remarkable sculpture depicts the four Aymon brothers fleeing the wrath of Charlemagne aboard their sturdy steed Bayard.

Follow the N92 out of Namur.

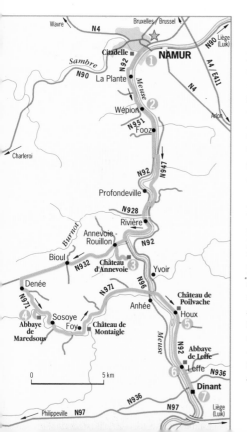

2 WÉPION

The Meuse is lined with weirs, one of the biggest being outside Namur, at La Plante. A few kilometres further is Wépion, a sleepy riverside village and Belgium's 'Strawberry Capital'. In summer, Wépion's shops sell vast quantities of their local pride and joy.

After Wépion, cross by the next bridge to the right bank, on to the N947. Passing opposite the water- and jet-ski centre at Profondeville, cross the river again at the next bridge and follow the winding N92 to Annevoie-Rouillon, then the signs for

'Jardins d'Annevoie' (Gardens of Annevoie).

3 CHÂTEAU D'ANNEVOIE

The 18th-century gardens of the château are among the wonders of Belgium, rivalling Tivoli's Villa d'Este in invention if not in scale. Water is the principal motif, channelled from the Annevoie stream to well up in fish-ponds, canals and fountains. Black swans cruise the ponds, and the château's impressive dimensions are reflected on the surface. Dazzling floral displays complete the picture.

Return to the N932 and drive for 7km before turning left, through Denée, to the Abbaye de Maredsous (Maredsous Abbey).

4 MAREDSOUS ABBEY

Set in rugged countryside in an area of stone-built villages, the abbey's twin towers dominate the skyline. Famed for its beer, cheese and bread (all of which can be sampled in the grounds) the Benedictine abbey has not neglected its religious reputation either. The abbey is surprisingly busy, especially at weekends, when the monks are vastly outnumbered by visitors refreshing their spirits in the open air.

Return to the Meuse via Sosoye, past the hilltop ruins of Château de Montaigle (Montaigle Castle), towards Anhée.

5 HOUX

Crossing to the right bank of the Meuse at Anhée, it is a short drive to Houx where the medieval ruins of Château de Poilvache overlook the river.

The N92 now follows the right bank. Stay on it until Leffe.

6 LEFFE

The Abbaye de Leffe (Leffe Abbey) just

outside Dinant is another of the many Belgian abbeys that somehow combine their spiritual calling with the brewing of beer, in this case the potent Leffe brew.

Continue on the N92 to Dinant.

7 DINANT

A bustling resort, Dinant, like many riverside towns, has a powerful and ancient Citadelle (Citadel), testifying to the perennial tramp of invading armies in the Meuse Valley (see pages 110–11). Dinant's troubled past includes one episode when its citizens were tied up in pairs and thrown from the Citadel into the river by a particularly ill-tempered conqueror. More encouragingly, Dinant has the strikingly handsome Collégiale Nôtre-Dame (Church of Our Lady) by the riverside and is a good place for shopping, particularly for the local hand-beaten copperware known as *dinanderie* and its pictorial gingerbreads (*couques*).

Strawberries are the big attraction in the riverside village of Wépion

Along the River Scheldt

This tour route follows the River Schelde/ River Escaut (River Scheldt), whose name changes as it crosses Belgium's Dutch/French language divide. Beginning at historic Ghent (see pages 78–9), the route ends at even more historic Tournai (see pages 116–17). On the way, it passes through characteristic small villages and farmland dotted with old châteaux. *Allow 4 hours for the drive.*

Begin the tour at Exit 15 (Ghent/Oudenaarde) on the E40 Brussels–Oostende motorway. Take the N60 in the direction of Oudenaarde and, after 1km, turn left on to the N469 towards Merelbeke. Continue over the Scheldt and turn right at the lights, following the sign for Gavere.

1 MERELBEKE TO SEMMERZAKE

After a few kilometres you reach the village of Schelderode. To your right are the polder-like fields of the Scheldt flood plain. As with most little villages along this rural road, Schelderode's most notable feature is its church, the 14th-century Sint-Martinuskerk.

The road continues through Melsen, Vurste, whose Kasteel Borgwal (Borgwal Castle) is now a residential home for handicapped people, and Semmerzake.

At Semmerzake, take the right fork, towards Eke, downhill to the Scheldt. Turn left before the bridge, towards Gavere.

2 SEMMERZAKE TO GAVERE

This narrow lower loop contrasts with the straighter high road, winding through tiny riverside villages and past the red-tiled roofs of numerous farmhouses. River barges may be seen

plying between Ghent and Tournai.
Skirt Gavere's shopping centre on the one-
way street which ends beside the river. Turn
left before the bridge and continue uphill
through the town.

3 GAVERE TO OUDENAARDE
Open countryside around Dikkelvenne
contrasts with the tight riverside fields.
Beerlegem is a steep-hilled village that
packs the 17th-century Sint-
Andreaskerk (Saint Andrew's Church)
and an 18th-century convent and castle
into its minuscule area.
Drive downhill past the church for 1km,
then turn right towards Paulatem. The
country lane ends at Sint-Maria-Latem.
Turn right and follow the N46 for 9km
through Nederzwalm to Oudenaarde, where
you follow the signs for Centrum (Centre) to
the Stadhuis, the richly decorated 16th-
century Town Hall.

4 OUDENAARDE
Oudenaarde (see page 75) compares
favourably with smaller Flemish cities
like Leuven and Mechelen. On what is
really a country drive, however, it
presents the problem of navigating busy
streets yet makes a convenient break for
a snack in one of the cafés on the Markt
(Main Square), followed by a stroll
around the Stadhuis (Town Hall).
From the Markt, follow signs for 'Andere
Richtingen' (Other Directions), then for
Ronse for 1km before turning right towards
Kluisbergen on the N8.

5 OUDENAARDE TO KLUISBERGEN
The landscape on your left begins to
climb towards the low hills of the
Vlaamse Ardennen (Flemish Ardennes).
This may be a geographical
exaggeration, but the wooded hills are
attractive enough.
In Kluisbergen, at the end of the N8, a
left turn is quickly followed by a right,
signposted for Ruien.

6 KLUISBERGEN TO ESCANAFFLES
This stretch passes beneath the Mont de
l'Enclus, a 145m-high hill overlooking
the Scheldt Valley. Between Ruien and
Escanaffles, you cross from Flanders to
Wallonia, but there is not much
evidence of this in the scenery.
At Escanaffles, follow the sign for Tournai.

7 ESCANAFFLES TO MONT-SAINT-AUBERT
A succession of roadside hamlets, such
as Pottes and Hérinnes, are separated by
fields. Lanes branch off towards rustic
farmhouses, while traffic is occasionally
slowed by a tractor or a hay wagon.
Three kilometres beyond Hérinnes, just
before Obigies, turn left, following the
'Panorama' sign, on to Rue du Vieux
Comté, and go straight on, following the
signs for Mont-Saint-Aubert. Keep straight
on at La Grignotière restaurant then turn
right at the roadside shrine. This road leads
past the Nature Park of Mont-Saint-
Aubert and arrives in Tournai.

The River Scheldt

Mineral Springs of Spa

This energetic walk takes you to the source of the European spa tradition, the numerous mineral springs around Spa, an attractive town set among the Ardennes hills and forests (see page 98). Spa was particularly popular during the 19th century, but notables (including Henry VIII and Tsar Peter the Great) have been taking the waters here for centuries. *Allow 4 hours minimum.*

Begin at Place Royale. There are several points along the way where you can 'abandon' the walk and return to Spa by bus.

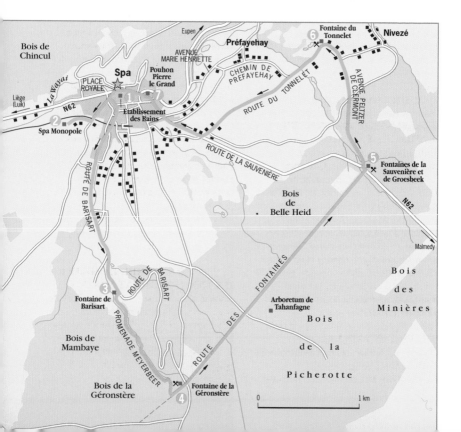

1 ETABLISSEMENT DES BAINS (BATHS ESTABLISHMENT)

The neo-classical Baths was the focal point of the Victorian-period mineral springs resort. Inside, except at weekends, it is possible to take a bath in naturally carbonated water from the nearby Hautes Fagnes Nature Reserve (see pages 102 and 120–1). Beside the Baths are the Casino and the Theatre.

From Place Royale, take Rue Albin Body, then Rue Auguste Laporte.

2 SPA MONOPOLE

The severely utilitarian bottling plant of the Spa Monopole company stands in harsh contrast to the elegant town whose prosperity it ensures. Guided tours are available daily.

Backtrack to Place Royale, then take Place Verte, Place de la Providence and Rue de Barisart. Continue for about 45 minutes, now on Route de Barisart, to the Fontaine de Barisart (Barisart Spring).

3 FONTAINE DE BARISART (BARISART SPRING)

This spring is the source of the commercially bottled Spa Barisart, which is also used in the baths at the Thermal Establishment in town. There is a cafeteria where you can relax before going downstairs to the spring for a cup of refreshing water.

A yellow sign for 'Promenade Meyerbeer' points up though the forest to the Fontaine de la Geronstère (Geronstère Spring), a 30-minute walk. As there are numerous promenades in the forest, it is important to follow the correct sign.

4 FONTAINE DE LA GERONSTÈRE (GERONSTÈRE SPRING)

This spring is located in a stone-built grotto in the gardens of a restaurant, also called La Geronstère, in an area with pleasant walks in the forests.

Follow the signs for Sauvenière. A 30-minute walk on the main road that runs through the forest, past the notable tree collection of the Arboretum de Tahanfagne, leads to the Fontaine de la Sauvenière (La Sauvenière Spring).

5 FONTAINE DE LA SAUVENIÈRE (SAUVENIÈRE SPRING)

The Fontaine de la Sauvenière and Fontaine de Groesbeek (Groesbeek Spring) are situated side by side in a downstairs vault next to another fine restaurant, also called La Sauvenière.

Continue downhill on Avenue Peltzer de Clermont for 30 minutes, to the Fontaine du Tonnelet (Tonnelet Spring).

6 FONTAINE DU TONNELET (TONNELET SPRING)

The other springs have all had Belgian restaurants located beside them, but at this one the restaurant La Fontaine du Tonnelet is Italian and based on a Tuscan country villa. Its exterior is painted in the same red-and-white colour scheme as the adjacent pavilion, where a spring emerges.

Continue downhill on Route du Tonnelet, then right on to Route de la Sauvenière, back to Spa.

7 POUHON PIERRE LE GRAND (PETER THE GREAT SPRING)

Back in Spa, on the way to Place Royale, is an airy pavilion which once doubled as a winter garden, called the Pouhon Pierre le Grand. For a few francs you can drink as much of the rather smelly but supposedly healthful water as you want.

THE FRANKS

One of the Germanic tribes that hovered on the Roman Empire's Rhine frontier, the Franks seized any opportunity to break in, plunder, and eventually settle. By the 5th century AD they were established in Belgium's Ardennes and Kempen, and when the Rhine defences were breached in 406 they joined the Germanic surge across western Europe.

It would have been small compensation to the traumatised citizenry to know that the Frankish barbarians scorching their land would give rise to a new civilization. Under the fierce King Childéric and his son Clovis, they set up their capital at Tournai in Belgium (see pages 116–17) in 446, but Clovis later moved it to Paris.

Childéric's burial chamber was discovered by chance in 1653 by a Tournaisien tradesman renovating his home, and a rich treasure, including a 'hive' of golden bees, was removed to Paris. Archaeologists have recently uncovered another chamber, containing the king's horses.

Even in puppet form, Charlemagne personifies the Holy Roman Empire

The Franks' power reached its zenith under Charlemagne, who was born in the Ardennes, probably at Liège, in 742. He ruled a kingdom covering France, Belgium, Luxembourg, the Netherlands, Germany, Austria and half of Italy. This encompassed most of the old Roman Empire in the West, a fact recognised by Pope Leo III, who crowned Charlemagne Holy Roman Emperor in 800.

Charlemagne's legacy remains in the Carolingian Renaissance in European thought, and in the romantic story of his chief paladin, Roland, killed fighting the Moors at the Battle of Roncesvalles, and whose legend lives on in the *Chanson de Roland*.

The Holy Roman Empire would prove to be part reality and part myth, but it was an ideal that ended only with the death of the Austro–Hungarian (Habsburg) Empire after World War I. Or did it? Charlemagne would undoubtedly recognise the European Union and share its vision of encompassing the entire continent.

GETTING AWAY FROM IT ALL

'In Flanders' fields the poppies blow,
Between the crosses, row on row,
That mark our place; and in the sky,
The larks, still bravely singing, fly.
Scarce heard amid the guns below.

We are the dead. Short days ago
We lived, felt dawn, saw sunset glow,
Loved, and were loved. And now we lie
In Flanders' fields.'

CANADIAN COLONEL JOHN MCCRAE
(1914–18)

Ardennes Adventure

*T*he Ardennes region is Belgium's holiday playground, even more so than the coast in some respects because the leisure possibilities are more varied. Some people go there to experience nature, some for the food, some for tranquillity and some for the adventure sports activities.

CANOEING AND KAYAKING

Ardennes rivers such as the Amblève, Our, Ourthe, Semois and Lesse are wildly popular with learner canoeists and kayakers. There are not many waterfalls and rapids – although they do exist – but in spring, when the Ardennes snows melt, the water can often be rough enough for 'Sunday canoeist' companies to suspend activities, and white-water enthusiasts come into their own.

The descent of the River Lesse in particular has become a rite of passage for teenagers; also for mums and dads aiming to give their children a taste of adventure and who do not mind getting wet all over in the process. Crowds of the already wet gather at strategic points on the route to cheer as other unfortunates come tumbling out of their canoes when the going gets tough. *Further information from the tourist offices listed below under Skiing.*

MOUNTAIN-BIKING

Much of the Ardennes terrain is perfectly suited to mountain-biking, which, after all, is scarcely possible in real mountains. Rough hills, narrow forest trails, unbridged streams exist all over the Ardennes and make tough courses for enthusiasts.

The East Cantons, Spa, La Roche-en-Ardenne and Durbuy are just a few areas where mountain-biking routes and cycle-hire are readily available. *For further information: see under Skiing (opposite) for sources.*

ROCK-CLIMBING

Although the Ardennes do not have mountains in the alpine sense of the term, there are some testing cliff-faces, particularly in the River Meuse valley. The Belgian army's élite para-commandos practise their mountaineering skills here, as do many ordinary enthusiasts.

On any weekend, the sheer cliffs at Anseremme near Dinant present the sight of little dots of bright colour against the grey rock, as climbers work their way up towards the dramatic view from the summit. *Further information from: Liège Province and Namur Province Tourist Office (see page 189 for addresses and telephone numbers).*

Canoeing on the River Lesse is a popular form of 'relaxation' in the Ardennes

SKIING

Both downhill and cross-country skiing are possible in the Ardennes, with 12 downhill and more than 80 cross-country locations. Toboggan and snow-scooter pistes also exist. The only problem is one that occasionally bedevils even alpine ski resorts: the unpredictability of snow.

Being at a much lower altitiude than the Alps (Belgium's highest point is 694m above sea level), the chance of no snow is greater. On the plus side, when there is snow, the Ardennes are easily accessible and a skiing break can be had at short notice and with little of the fuss that attends an expedition to the Alps. Ski equipment can be hired from sports shops and hotels in the skiing areas.

The Hautes Fagnes Nature Reserve (see pages 102, 120–1) represents some of the best cross-country skiing, but this is a sensitive environmental zone and it is illegal to ski off the authorised pistes. *Snow reports and additional information are available from the Touring Club (tel: (02) 233 2490), and from the Belgian National Tourist Office, which also publishes an annual brochure called* Ski Ardennes, *the tourist offices of Liège, Namur and Luxembourg provinces and of the East Cantons (see page 189 for addresses, etc).*

SKYDIVING AND PARACHUTING

The aerodrome at La Sauvenière outside Spa, as well as offering sightseeing flights, has a parachuting and skydiving school attached. There are chalets, a camping ground and parking space for camper-vans. Instruction is offered to beginners, and more experienced skydivers can also jump from here. *Further information from: Aerodrome de Spa–La Sauvenière, Route de la Sauvenière (tel: aerodrome (087) 771976; para-club (087) 774183).*

> ### RIVERS OF THE ARDENNES
>
> It could be argued that there is only one real river in the Ardennes, the River Meuse (see pages 110–11), whose stately progress has made it a highway of history, commerce and tourism. Once into the rugged Ardennes countryside, however, you find many streams, none of which really merit their description as 'rivers', but which compensate with picturesque courses through steep, winding valleys.
>
> The Amblève, Our, Ourthe, Semois and Lesse are the most important arenas for canoeing, fishing and swimming, and scenic riverside routes for mountain-bike tours and hikes (see pages 128–9).
>
> Each has its own character: the Amblève (called the Amel for part of its length), slicing through the valley below the Hautes Fagnes; the Our, which follows the border with Germany then runs into Luxembourg; the Ourthe taking the Ardennes by the waist; the wild loops of the Semois; and the kayaker's testing ground of the Lesse.
>
> Many Ardennes towns and villages owe their isolation or the drama of their location to the rivers that flow through them. It would be hard to imagine Bouillon or La Roche or Durbuy anywhere else than on the banks of a fast-flowing stream.
>
> If it should seem that the 'big five' have acquired a little too much popularity, there is always another stream just over the next hill. The Aisne, Houille, Hoyoux, Lienne, Lomme, Salm, Sûre, Vesdre, Vire, Warche, Weser, Wimbre and Ywoigne all have their moments too.

CANAL BOATS

Belgium has an extensive network of rivers and canals, leading to the European waterway network. So many barges ply to and from Antwerp and other ports that they have to be berthed in great 'parking lots' and there are traffic jams at the busiest intersections. While the merchant marine carries the red, yellow and black ensign to Yokohama and New York, the bargemen settle modestly for Basle and Budapest.

the countryside, dish antennae trained on the nearest TV satellite, a car ready for use on deck, net curtains on the pilot-house windows and warm lights behind the ports.

Some barge families still live on the water, but intense competition from road and rail freight has put heavy pressure on the small operators. The new-style barges are big, powerful and expensive; operating costs are always on the owners' minds and so the romantic days of the canal and river families are probably numbered.

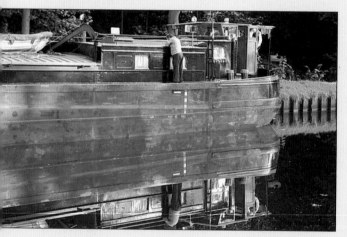

They can still be seen, however, at places like the Schippers Beurs (Shippers Exchange) in Antwerp, a temple of commerce that witnessed the days when many barges were pulled by a man in harness walking along the towpath. Although most cargoes are allocated by long-term contracts, some are still chalked up on the Exchange's boards and barge skippers stand around deciding which ones to take.

The Rivers Scheldt and Meuse, and the Albert and Central Canals, are hard-working bodies of water, their surfaces furrowed with the luminous tracks of heavily laden barges coming and going from Antwerp, Ghent and Zeebrugge to the inland ports of Europe. The black-and-white-painted boats can be seen thrumming through

Big or small, the barges carry with them their own unique selling point: the heaviest and often the nastiest cargoes.

Canal barges are big business, not just a nostalgic form of transport

National Parks

*A*lthough not possessing national parks on the scale of America's Yellowstone, Belgium has its share of protected landscapes and habitats. If anything, the preservation of open spaces and wildlife areas in a small, densely populated country acquires greater importance.

The biggest is the Hautes Fagnes Nature Park (see pages 102 and 120–1), which combines with Germany's Eifel Park to form a cross-border protected zone. Although development is moderated throughout the park, only the Hautes Fagnes Nature Reserve section is completely controlled. Belgium's highest point is here in this wild area of high, boggy fenland.

The Zwin Nature Reserve (see page 72) at the coast is a key stopover and breeding place for birds, both migrating and indigenous species. Binoculars, which can be hired at the visitor centre, will get you close enough to the antics of our avian friends, as the breeding areas are out of bounds. The coast also has extensive dunes areas in the Zandpanne Dunes Reserve and the Westhoek Nature Reserve.

Temptation is dinner beyond reach for this heron fishing in a tranquil national park

In the Ardennes, the Lesse and Lomme National Park includes some spectacular scenery around the two rivers of the same name, a Wild Animal Reserve and the caves at Han (see page 96). Outside Liège, on the River Meuse, the Sart Tilman Natural Park forms part of the campus of Liège University.

There are many others scattered around the country, ranging down to less than a hectare in size. They protect lakes, rivers, woods and forests, heathland, dunes, cliffs, marshes, caves, and the habitats of endangered or rare wildlife and plant species.

Visitor information can be obtained from provincial tourist offices (see page 190). Public access may be restricted, or denied completely, at certain times and in certain areas. Park rangers enforce these regulations energetically, always mindful of the damage that can be done by human activity in sensitive natural environments.

DIRECTORY

'There was a sound of revelry by night,
And Belgium's capital had gather'd then
Her Beauty and her Chivalry, and bright
the lamps shone o'er fair women and brave men'.

LORD BYRON
Childe Harold, (1816)

Shopping

Speciality products often have a regional or local origin, but are generally available throughout the country. It can add to the interest to a visit to buy at the source, but other factors, such as price and transportation, may in the end take priority.

Ceramics

Brussels-based workshops produce a wide range of ceramics, ranging from the utilitarian to the artistic. The Ardennes village of La Roche-en-Ardenne has also gained a reputation for the quality of its pottery.

Crystal

Many Belgian shop-windows feature dazzling displays of crystal. The name to watch for is Val-Saint-Lambert, founded in 1826, whose workshop outside Liège (see page 109) produces hand-carved, blown-glass pieces of outstanding quality, some of which are very expensive, as well as more 'ordinary' and affordable items. Other makes may not be as prestigious as Val-Saint-Lambert but together they create a wide range of choice.

Romancing the stones that earn Antwerp a sparkling $16 billion a year

Diamonds

Antwerp's diamond industry accounts for $16 billion a year and almost half the world's polished diamond sales – so the merchants in the Diamond Quarter (see page 61) must be doing something right. Just visiting the Quarter is a fascinating experience, and the 'Antwerp cut' is said to give the precious stones more sparkle.

Diamonds are, however, expensive items. The people who deal in them are very careful about values and it is right that buyers should be also. There are various ways of gaining knowledge to make an informed choice, and sales-oriented tours are not necessarily the best way.

That said, the quantity of stones and the level of competition (although neither is allowed to become excessive) ensure that fair deals are the norm. But bargains are not to be expected.

Dinanderie

Originating in and around the River Meuse town of Dinant (see page 110) *dinanderie* is hand-beaten copper or bronze which in centuries past was used for religious vessels and decorative work for churches. Today, its uses are more worldly, but a cottage industry of local artisans ensures that it bears the distinctive stamp of a venerable tradition.

Jewellery

Partly in combination with the diamond

industry, jewellery has become something of a Belgian speciality. Art schools, particularly but not exclusively in Antwerp and Brussels, are producing highly regarded young designers and artisans, some of whose work has received international recognition.

Lace

This is the product most commonly associated in visitors' minds with Belgium. This is partly due to the association with the medieval and Renaissance tradition of lace-making, and partly to sharp modern marketing and promotion. Lace is ubiquitous in Belgium; sadly, quality is not.

Most of the lace on sale is machine-made, and may even have been imported. This does not automatically mean 'bad', but it does mean that someone who thinks they are buying handmade Belgian lace with centuries of tradition behind it is liable to be disappointed. Such lace does exist, of course, and has a price-tag appropriate to its rarity (see pages 140–1).

Pewter

The River Meuse town of Huy (see page 111) is noted for its production of pewter and other tin-based products, not only jugs but ornaments and works of art.

Tapestry

This industry has a similar tale to that of lace (see above). The tradition continues, both in machine-made copies of old masterpieces and in the modern and often highly individualistic works of small-scale producers.

Beers, *geneva* (gin), chocolates and certain foodstuffs are also good buys.

Young Belgian jewellery designers have earned a growing international reputation

These have been included in the section on **Food and Drink** (pages 162–3 and 172–3) and are widely available throughout the country.

Quality and style are the trademark of Delvaux handbags

SHOPPING IN BRUSSELS

Brussels' commitment to the art of shopping goes back a long way. One of the first new buildings to grace the capital of independent Belgium was an elegant shopping gallery that is said to be Europe's first mall. Since then, several distinct shopping areas have developed, and the city has enough possibilities to keep even the most committed shopper busy.

CITY CENTRE

Galeries du Centre/Centrumgalerij

Leonidas has a shop here, selling superb Belgian chocolates.
Off Rue des Fripiers/Kleerkopersstraat.

Galerie Ravenstein/Ravensteingalerij

An airy and stylish mall that makes a pleasant place to shop.
Across from Central Station.

Galeries Royales Saint-Hubert/Koninklijke Sint-Hubertus Galerijen

Opened in 1847, the Italian neo-Renaissance-style galleries offer shopping with a touch of class. Among others, there are Oriande (crystal and jewellery) (tel: (02) 512 4932); Libraire des Galeries (books) (tel: (02) 511 2412); Ganterie Italienne (gloves) (tel: (02) 512 7538); Delvaux (handbags and leather goods) (tel: (02) 512 7198); and Neuhaus (chocolates) (tel: (02) 502 5914).
Between Rue du Marché-aux-Herbes/ Grasmarkt and Rue d'Arenberg/ Arenbergstraat.

Grand Place/Grote Markt

Belgian lace is sold, mostly in souvenir shops, here and on adjacent side-streets. Some, but not all, is handmade.

Rue Antoine Dansaert/Antoine Dansaertstraat

For stylish boutiques with a reputation for brashness: Della Spiga (tel: (02) 511 0901); Stijl (tel: (02) 512 0313). The streets adjacent to here have been developing into a mini-China Town, with supermarkets and restaurants.
Across from the Bourse/Beurs (Stock Exchange).

Rue des Fripiers/Kleerkopersstraat

Ragazzi (tel: (02) 218 8216) and Kookaï (tel: (02) 218 6729) are fashionable clothes boutiques; In Den Olifant (tel: (02) 217 4397) is a twee but charming toy shop.
Adjacent to Place de la Monnaie/ Muntplein.

Rue au Beurre/Boterstraat

Dandoy (tel: (02) 511 0326) is the place for sweet-toothed biscuit fans; try *speculoos* and *pain à grecque*.
Behind the Stock Exchange.

Rue du Midi/Zuidstraat

Stamps and coins dealers line part of this street as well as some offbeat specialty shops.
Adjacent to the Bourse/Beurs (Stock Exchange).

PORTE DE NAMUR/ NAAMSEPOORT

This is the main up-market shopping district, and includes adjacent streets and galleries running as far as Avenue Louise/Louizalaan and Place Stéphanie/Stefanieplein.

Avenue Louise/Louizalaan

Olivier Strelli (tel: (02) 511 4383), the Belgian fashion designer, is just one of several designers with boutiques here.

Near the Place Stéphanie/Stefanieplein end of the avenue.

Boulevard de Waterloo/Waterloolaan

For Gucci (tel: (02) 511 1182), Gianni Versace(tel: (02) 511 8559), Nina Ricci (tel: (02) 512 5836) and others of the same type.

Malls

A maze of glittering malls leads off the streets in this area: Galerie Louise/ Louizagalerij, Galerie Porte de Namur/ Naamsepoortgalerij and Galerie de la Toison d'Or/Guldenvliesgalerij. Prices are high.

RUE NEUVE/NIEUWSTRAAT

The area around this street is popular in terms of choice and keen prices. It includes a number of malls and adjoining streets.

Boulevard Adolphe Max/Adolphe Maxlaan

Has a wide range of shops, including some slightly up-market clothes shops. W H Smith, the British bookshop chain (tel: (02) 219 2708), has a branch here. *Parallel to Rue Neuve/Nieuwstraat.*

Centre Monnaie/Muntcentrum and Anspach Center

Two malls with shops similar to City 2 (see below).
Place de la Monnaie/Muntplein and Boulevard Anspach/Anspachlaan.

City 2

Almost every type of shop is together under one roof in this multi-storey mall. FNAC, a good-value books, electronics and photo shop, has a branch here (tel: (02) 209 2211) (it also sells concert tickets); as has Inno, Belgium's main department store chain (tel: (02) 211 2111).
Rue Neuve/Nieuwstraat and Boulevard du Jardin Botanique/Kruidtuinstraat.

Rue Neuve/Nieuwstraat

A long, narrow, busy pedestrian precinct lined with clothing stores, electrical goods shops, department stores, etc. The biggest choice and keenest prices are to be found here.

GRAND SABLON/GROTE ZAVEL

This attractive cobbled square (and to a lesser extent its neighbour, the Petit Sablon/Kleine Zavel) has an important concentration of art and antiques shops – with a pricey reputation.

WOLUWE

Of the several suburban shopping centres, this has the best reputation. It has many of the shops that can be found in the city, but without the aggravation of busy traffic, except on a Saturday.
Metro: Roodebeek.

Stylish shopping is the rule rather than the exception in Brussels

LACE

Look in the Brussels *Yellow Pages* directory under Dentelles/Kantwerk (Lace) and you will find about 40 listings. Had there been a *Yellow Pages* in the 17th century, there would have been some 22,000, the estimated number of lace-makers in that city alone.

Belgium was where Europe's rich and famous bought lace, so much so that in 1662 the British Parliament, concerned at the vast sums being expended, banned its importation. Belgian rulers also intervened, as in the 1590 Edict of Ghent, when the Emperor Philip II forbade girls over 12 to make lace. Neither government's

interference had much effect.

The handmade threadwork of silk, linen or cotton seems to have originated around the start of the 16th century, either in Venice or in the Flemish weaving cities. This original type, known as needle-point lace, uses threads as a framework to which stitches are fastened in loops.

A later form, bobbin lace, certainly began in Flanders and uses pins around which threads are crossed and braided. Both techniques required great delicacy, skill and concentration to achieve the results seen in

Renaissance portraits of wealthy individuals wearing gauzey dresses and ruffs of lace.

As well as Brussels, other Belgian towns produced lace to which a distinct local style was added. Mechelen, for example, developed the *ijsgrond* (ice-field) style, a small hexagonal stitch of such intricacy that Mechelen lace became both greatly desired and very expensive. Bruges, Antwerp, Binche, Turnhout, Poperinge and Sint-Truiden were also centres of lace production. Fashion has passed lace by, but it is still sought after for baptismal dress and ornamental use. Although most is machine-produced, handmade lace can still be found and some shops deal only in the handmade product. There is a slow revival of the painstaking skills that can create dainty works of art out of thread.

A delicate touch is the essential ingredient of the finest lace

SHOPPING OUTSIDE THE CAPITAL

Brussels is far from being the only important shopping city in Belgium. Antwerp would give little away in any competition over style and range of facilities with the capital, and the same holds true for Liège.

Most of the seaside towns look on shopping as an extension of tourism, with Sunday shopping a frequent option. Knokke–Heist stands out in this respect, particularly for its many (and usually expensive) clothes boutiques. Ghent, Bruges, Tournai and Namur tend to be more mixed, with tourist-oriented shopping alongside 'ordinary' facilities for their residents.

Outlying areas usually have a shopping focus in the main town: Hasselt, and to a lesser extent Turnhout, fulfil this purpose in the Kempen, but there is really no equivalent in the Ardennes, although Spa, Eupen and

Bastogne would come closest (as well as Liège, of course).

A feature of modern shopping trends is the 'ribbon development' along major roads out of Brussels, Antwerp and some other cities, usually for large purchases like furniture. In the border areas, particularly near Luxembourg, such developments are more widely based, catering for different price levels between countries.

The bigger department and chain stores, such as Inno, FNAC and Blokker, are usually represented in the bigger towns.

ANTWERP

The city's principal mainstream shopping district is the street called the Meir, and the surrounding area. For more touristy or history-oriented items, the maze of narrow streets around the cathedral contains many interesting shops.

Antwerp offers shoppers more than diamonds

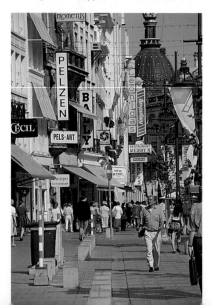

Balloons

A shop that delivers on the promise of its name, with little in the way of hot air. All kinds of party balloonery.
Bredebaan 148, Brasschaat (tel: (03) 653 1515).

Cinderella

Fashion, style and the kind of clothing that Cinderella might have worn to the disco.
Melkmart 2 (tel: (03) 233 4018).

Dille en Kamille

Natural foods and household articles that go along with that lifestyle.
Vleminckstraat 9 (tel: (03) 234 3208).

Extra Large

Either a brilliant idea, or a case of

megalomania. Extra Large takes all kinds of things, from trinkets to household articles, and 'blows them up' to impressive, or senseless, proportions. Take your pick.
Oude Beurs 30 (tel: (03) 232 9841).

Jazz Corner
Also includes blues in the stock of its otherwise one-track speciality.
Kerkstraat 80a (tel: (03) 236 0971).

Huis Van De Voorde
Not selling one of the most politically correct products on the market, perhaps, but its astonishing range of pipe, tobacco and cigar lines are a reminder of the days when smoking could be considered a connoisseur's art.
Lange Koepoortstraat 43–9 (tel: (03) 232 0167).

BRUGES
Steenstraat and Zuidzandstraat are the main shopping streets, with souvenir, lace and small specialty shops to be found all over the centre.

Verheecke
For homemade pralines.
Steenstraat 30 (tel: (050) 332286).

Artlux
Leather goods such as handbags and gloves.
Simon Stevinplein 1 (tel: (050) 336095).

A M Fimmers & L V der Cruysse
Antiques and domestic silver.
Sint-Salvatorskerkhof 18 (tel: (050) 342025).

GHENT
Many regular shops are clustered on and around the street called Langemunt,

which runs parallel to the River Leie in the city centre.

Chocolatier Van Hecke
You might say that this is a heck of a good chocolate shop, and in Belgium that is no mean praise. Its speciality is handmade pralines.
Koestraat 42 (tel: (09) 225 4357).

Cockney's Distillery
Noted for selling its own fruit-enhanced *jenever (geneva* – see page 173), which makes a fine Belgian gift in an attractive bottle.
Drongensesteenweg 140 (tel: (09) 2262880).

Giochi Sobrie
Toys, but the kind of toys Santa used to bring long before the computer chip was invented: music boxes, wooden clowns and animals, tin soldiers.
Henegouwenstraat 6 (tel: (09) 224 2620).

Tierentyn
A shop that is as keen as mustard on … mustard. Homemade and sold in an olde worlde ambience.
Groentenmarkt 3 (tel: (09) 225 8336).

LIÈGE
Most department stores, clothes shops, etc, are to be found in the extensive shopping area close to the cathedral.

MARKETS

Many Belgians rarely seem happier than when they are wandering around one of the enormous number of markets, whose stalls must cover a sizeable percentage of this small country's land area. Permanent markets, travelling markets, specialty markets, antique markets, flea markets, animal markets, fish markets – all add up to a market economy *par excellence*.

ANTWERP
Antiques Market

Includes a great deal of material that might be better classified as 'jumble', but there are also genuine antiques.
Lijnwaardmarkt (near the cathedral). Every Saturday from Easter to October, 9am–5pm.

Rubens Market

Takes place only one day a year, when stallholders dress up in 17th-century costume to sell their wares.
Grote Markt. August 15, all day.

Birds Market

Despite its name, game and poultry are no longer the only things sold here. In fact, just about anything that can be carried is for sale. An 'Exotic Market' takes place in the same location every Saturday.
Oude Vaartplaats/Theaterplein. Sunday 8.30am–1pm; Saturday 9am–4pm.

Friday Market

Has a slightly misleading name because the market also takes place on Wednesday – in the Vrijdagmarkt (Friday Market Square). It deals in antiques, household goods and second-hand furniture sold by auction.
Vrijdagmarkt. Wednesday and Friday 8am–1pm.

BRUGES
Antiques and Flea Market

A superb setting on a tree-shaded canalside in the city centre makes this a visual experience as well as a source of good buys.
Dijver. 1 April to 30 September, Saturday and Sunday, all day.

Vrijdagmarkt (Friday Market)

Despite its name, this general market is no longer held on Friday, but on Saturday, in the same square where the centuries-old Friday Market used to be held.
't Zand. Saturday 8am–noon.

BRUSSELS
Antiques Market

An excellent if somewhat pricey weekend antiques market, with knowledgeable and enthusiastic stallholders. Held in one of Brussels' most beautiful old squares.
Place du Grand-Sablon/Grote Zavelplein. Saturday 9am–6pm; Sunday 9am–2pm.

Bird Market

If birds for sale (many with their wings clipped so they cannot fly) interest you, the place to be is the Main Square every Sunday.
Grand-Place/Grote Markt. Sunday 7am–2pm.

Crafts Market

Jewellery, ornaments and other designer bric-à-brac are sold in a relaxed ambience in one of Brussels' central squares.
Place de l'Agora/Agoraplein. Saturday and Sunday 10am–6pm.

Flea Market

Perhaps Brussels' most interesting market, and a slice of city life that is light years from the smooth Euro-city image fostered by the powers that be. The flea market is held in the poor but spirited Marolles district and just about anything that it is possible to imagine can be bought.
Place du Jeu de Balle/Vossenplein. Daily 7am–2pm.

Flower Market

A long-time Brussels tradition, the Flower Market is not large, but it is colourful.
Grand-Place/Grote Markt. Tuesday to Sunday 8am–6pm.

Midi Market

All kinds of ordinary goods, clothes and foodstuffs at extraordinarily cheap prices.
Around the Midi/Zuid (South) Railway Station. Sunday 5am–1pm.

LIBRAMONT

Foire Agricole de Libramont (Libramont Agricultural Fair)

The pride of Belgian agriculture goes on display here, such as prize-winning examples of the *Bleu-Blanc Belge* (Belgian Blue-White) beef cattle and the *Brabantse trekpaarden* (Brabant draughthorses). Even non-farmers should have a fascinating day out.
Libramont village. Every July, for four days towards the end of the month.

Sunday antiques market in Spa

LIÈGE

La Batte Market

A famous mixed market that attracts bargain hunters from France, Germany, Holland and Luxembourg. It extends for several kilometres along the left bank of the River Meuse.
Quai de la Batte/Quai de Maestricht. Sunday 8am–2pm.

SPA

Antiques and Bric-à-Brac Market

Held in a wrought-iron colonnaded gallery, adjoining the elegant Parc de Sept Heures, the market is a curious mix of fine antiques and old rubbish.
Galerie Léopold II. Sunday 8am–2pm.

Entertainment

*B*elgian towns and cities may be geographically close, but they are far from identical in their definition of 'a good time'. Eating and drinking are common threads throughout, as is an extensively based and popularly received tradition in the performing arts.

Brussels, Antwerp, Ghent and Liège are the focus of all-round entertainment possibilities, but smaller cities and towns, like Namur, Charleroi, Leuven and Tournai are equipped with scaled-down versions of the same. Bruges, surprisingly enough, is not noted for its entertainment possibilities.

What's On information can be found in the weekly English-language magazine, *The Bulletin* and the cultural pages of the newspapers *Le Soir* and *De Standaard*, as well as local newspapers throughout the country. Provincial (see page 189) and local tourist offices publish magazines and/or brochures that give information on forthcoming events

CASINOS

These are particularly popular on the coast and in Meuse Valley resort towns.

Casino Blankenberge
Zeedijk 150, Blankenberge (tel: (050) 423020).

Casino de Chaudfontaine (outside Liège)
Esplanade 1, Chaudfontaine (tel: (041) 650753).

Casino de Dinant
Rue Grande 28, Dinant (tel: (082) 225894).

Casino Knokke
Zeedijk-Albertstrand 509, Knokke–Heist (tel: (050) 630500).

Casino Kursaal Oostende
Monacoplein-Oosthelling, Oostende (tel: (059) 705111).

Casino de Namur
Avenue Baron de Moreau 1, Namur (tel: (081) 220334).

Casino de Spa
Dating from 1763, the Casino is said to be the world's oldest.
Rue Royale 4, Spa (tel: (087) 772052).

CINEMA

Movies are popular in Belgium and even small towns have a cinema, while larger ones have several, usually grouped into multi-screen complexes. Most films are shown in the original language, with French and Dutch sub-titles. Brussels' **Bruparck** recreation centre (see pages 28–9) contains Kinepolis, which has 29 cinemas including an IMAX wrap-around screen, and claims to be the world's biggest cinema complex.

CLASSICAL MUSIC

Belgians' commitment to their orchestras and chamber music ensembles is second to none.

ANTWERP
DeSingel
A multi-form arts centre, which also features dance, opera and theatre.
Desguinlei 25 (tel: (03) 248 3800).

Koningin Elisabethzaal
A large venue often used for classical
concerts, and also for rock music and
theatre productions.
*Koningin Astridplein 26 (tel: (03) 233
8444).*

BRUSSELS
Cirque Royal/Koninklijk Circus
(Royal Circus)
For classical music, theatre, dance and
opera, and also occasional jazz and rock
performances.
*Rue de l'Enseignement/ Onderrichtsstraat
81 (tel: (02) 218 2015).*

Conservatoire Royal de Musique/
Koninklijk Muziekconservatorium
(Royal Music Conservatory)
The main venue for chamber music.
*Rue de la Régence/Regentschapsstraat 30
(tel: (02) 511 0427).*

Palais des Beaux-Arts/Paleis voor
Schone-Kunsten (Palace of Fine
Arts)
The city's main venue for classical
music, and home-base of the Belgian
National Orchestra.
*Rue Ravenstein/Ravensteinstraat 23
(tel: (02) 507 8200).*

LIÈGE
Conservatoire Royal de Musique
(Royal Music Conservatory)
Liège's main concert venue.
*Boulevard Piercot 27–9 (tel: (041)
220306).*

DISCOS AND CLUBS
The youth music scene is influential on a
European scale, being at the forefront of
the latest trends. It was in Belgian discos
and clubs that New Beat made its
appearance several years ago.

ANTWERP
Café d'Anvers
The Cafe d'Anvers is a rather stylish
disco which is frequented by Antwerp's
trend-setters.
Verversrui 15 (tel: (03) 226 3870).

Jimmy's
Jimmy's has an informal style that goes
with its name.
*Van Ertbornstraat 12 (tel: (03) 233
3515).*

New Casino
The New Casino is the venue to which
'30-somethings' come to dance. Sunday
evenings are the time for even older
swingers to enjoy themselves on the
dance floor.
Kloosterstraat 70 (tel: (03) 237 8846).

Dressed to thrill at Oostende's rather
unsavourily named Dead Rat's Ball

BRUSSELS
Cartagena
Hot-blooded Latin American disco.
Rue Marché au Charbon/Kolenmarkt 70 (no telephone).

Le Garage
Not as chic a disco as it once was, but every bit as gloomily atmospheric, and still a popular venue.
Rue Duquesnoy/Duquesnoystraat 16 (tel: (02) 512 6622).

Griffin's
A cocktails and smart dress kind of place.
Rue de l'Homme Chrétien/ Kerstenmannekensstraat 2 (tel: (02) 505 5200).

Mirano Continental
The smart set's favourite dancehall.
Chaussée de Louvain/Leuvensesteenweg 38 (tel: (02) 218 5772).

New Portland
Up-market dancing for the well off and well dressed.
Place de la Chapelle/Kapellemarkt 6 (no telephone).

Vaudeville
Located in the Royal Saint Hubert Galleries, this is a more restrained disco for dancers whose wildest days are a few years behind them.
Galerie de la Reine/Koningingalerij 15 (tel: (02) 512 4997).

GHENT
Barney'z
Even more fashion-conscious than the average disco, the aim at Barney'z is to be supercool despite the hot music and the crowds.
Muinkaai 1 (tel: (09) 251069).

Boccaccio
Puts itself at the forefront of the latest disco trends and charges for the privilege.
Solariumdreef 5, Destelbergen (tel: (09) 282414).

Champs Elysées
With the look of the belle époque, at least as far as the decor goes, Champs Elysées aims to bring a touch of French class to the music scene.
Citadellelaan 2 (tel: (09) 223250).

LIÈGE
La Chapelle
Only the latest sounds will do for a disco aimed directly at Liège's many students and other young people out for a wild evening on the town.
Rue Chapelle Clercs 3 (tel: (041) 232685).

Palace Club
Young and stylish location that appeals to the more classically minded (in disco terms) dancers.
Place Saint-Paul 8 (tel: (041) 234053).

Upside
Lots of flashing lights, noise and a crowded dance-floor. In other words, a young person's disco heaven.
Rue de la Wache 13 (tel: (041) 231488).

LIVE MUSIC AND CABARET
Jazz is particularly popular.

ANTWERP
Carillon Concerts
From mid-June to mid-September these are played from the Cathedral of Our Lady (see pages 60–1). Popular 'listening places' are the café terraces around the Grote Markt.

De Muze
Jazz features frequently on the programme of this café.
Melkmarkt 15 (tel: (03) 226 0126).

Swingcafé
Traditional café which features regular performances of live jazz.
Suikerrui 13 (tel: (03) 233 1478).

BRUSSELS
Black Bottom
Raffish, Parisienne-style piano cabaret, whose languid hosts keep the show lazing along.
Rue du Lombard/Lombardstraat 1 (tel: (02) 511 0608).

Blues Corner
When the music is playing at full pelt, no one seems to notice how noisy, crowded, smoky and dark this place can be.
Rue des Chapeliers/Hoedenmakersstraat 12 (tel: (02) 511 9794).

Forest National
Rock concerts. Tickets available from FNAC department stores.
Avenue du Globe/Globelaan 36 (tel: (02) 347 0355).

Karaoke Bar
A well-dressed kind of place in the city's top Japanese hotel, the bar is popular with many – apart from the Japanese contingent.
Hotel Tagawa, Avenue Louise/Louizalaan 321–5 (tel: (02) 640 8029).

New York Café
A touch of class to go along with some cool, sophisticated jazz.
Place Stéphanie/Stefanieplein 5 (tel: (02) 534 8509).

Open-air jazz keeps Brussels in tune and provides music for all

Preservation Hall
A slightly down-at-heel jazz bar that compensates with top-notch jazz in the style of its New Orleans namesake.
Rue de Londres/Londenstraat 3 (tel: (02) 502 1597).

LIÈGE
Caves de Porto
An ambience-rich jazz location on one of Liège's oldest streets.
En Féronstrée 144 (tel: (041) 232325).

Le Lion S'En Vole
A top spot for jazz.
Rue Roture 11 (tel: (041) 410244).

NIGHTCLUBS
Nightclubs are not a very highly developed entertainment form in Belgium.

BRUSSELS
Show Point
Lots of glitter, not much in the way of clothes, and an expense account might come in handy.
14 Place Stéphanie/Stefanieplein 14 (tel: (02) 511 5364).

OPERA AND DANCE

Both types of company often share the same location.

ANTWERP

Koninklijke Vlaamse Opera (Royal Flemish Opera)

A superb old building, home of the Vlaamse Opera. The Koninklijk Ballet van Vlaanderen (Royal Flanders Ballet) also performs here.

Frankrijklei 3 (tel: (03) 233 6685).

BRUSSELS

Théâtre Royal de la Monnaie/ Koninklijke Muntschouwburg (Royal Mint Theatre)

Featuring both opera and dance in a superb and historic setting, the Mint is the city's cultural showpiece and home of the Royal Mint Opera. Maurice Béjart's Ballet du XXième Siècle (20th Century Ballet) and the Mark Morris Dance Company are two dance troupes that have been based here.

Place de la Monnaie/Muntplein (tel: (02) 229 1211).

CHARLEROI

Palais des Beaux-Arts (Palace of Fine Arts)

Home of the Ballet Royal de Wallonie (Royal Wallonia Ballet).

Place du Manege (tel: (071) 311 212).

GHENT

Koninklijke Opera (Royal Opera)

A key venue for the Festival of Flanders, and hosts frequent opera and ballet productions.

Schouwburgstraat 3 (tel: (09) 225 2425).

LIÈGE

Théâtre Royal (Royal Theatre)

Home of the Opera Royal de Wallonie (Royal Wallonia Opera).

Rue des Dominicains 1 (tel: (041) 214720).

THEATRE

A difficulty for foreigners may be that most productions are performed in either French or Flemish, although English performances do take place in some theatres.

ANTWERP

Arenberg Theater

Occasionally features English-language productions.

Arenbergstraat 28 (tel: (03) 202 4611).

Koninklijke Nederlandse Schouwburg (Royal Netherlandic Theatre)

Mostly Dutch-language performances take place here.

Theaterplein, Meistraat 2 (tel: (03) 231 9750).

BRUSSELS

Théâtre Royal du Parc/Koninklijke Parktheater (Royal Park Theatre)

The place to go to see mainstream theatre.

Rue de la Loi/Wetstraat 3 (tel: (02) 511 4147).

Théâtre Toone/Toonetheater (Theatre Toone)

A folklore puppet theatre attached to an old Brussels bar.

Petite Rue des Bouchers/ Kortebeenhouwersstraat 21 (tel: (02) 217 2753).

Théâtre Varia

Modern theatre and dance.

Rue du Sceptre/Skepterstraat 78 (tel: (02) 640 8258).

Cultural Festivals

*T*he annual Festival of Flanders and Festival of Wallonia feature some of the best Belgian and international orchestras, ballet troupes and opera companies. A highlight of their programme is the series of joint-venture 'Castle Concerts', which take place in Belgium's most beautiful castles.

FESTIVAL OF FLANDERS

Runs from April to October each year and places great stress on international co-productions. The enormous range of events and venues makes it impossible to follow everything, but if you are in Antwerp, Bruges, Brussels, Ghent, Kortrijk, Leuven, Mechelen or Tongeren during the Festival period, there is sure to be something on.
Programme from: Festival van Vlaanderen, Rue Ravenstein/Ravensteinstraat 60, 1000 Brussels (tel: (02) 548 9595).

FESTIVAL OF WALLONIA

Runs from mid-June to mid-October and combines seven local festivals: Hainaut, Huy–Durbuy, Liège, Luxembourg, Namur, Stavelot and Walloon Brabant. This tends to make its events smaller in scale than that of Flanders, and more likely to be found in out-of-the-way venues. Quality is not sacrificed, however, as choirs and chamber-music ensembles of international repute are featured.
Programme from: Festival de Wallonie, Rue de l'Armée Grouchy 20, 5000 Namur (tel: (081) 733781).

EUROPALIA

Putting culture into Brussels' status as Capital of Europe and celebrating the European ideal, Europalia is a biennial festival held in odd-numbered years. It features a selected country's full gamut of cultural expression: art, music, dance, poetry, etc. (A one-year delay in featuring Turkey means that the festival may move to even-numbered years.)

Europalia runs from September to December and the range of events, focused in Brussels but including venues throughout the country, can be truly staggering. Participation, once limited to European countries, has been widened. Japan and Mexico have also been selected.
Programme from: Europalia International Foundation, Rue Royale/Koningsstraat 10, 1000 Brussels (tel: (02) 507 8550).

Concert in the Palais Royal, Brussels

Folklore Festivals

*D*ressing as Inca deities; hurling cats from high buildings; walloping bystanders with inflated pigs' bladders; carrying the cross through the streets in penance; gathering in solemn conclave to honour a dish that looks suspiciously like a *croque monsieur* (a cheese-and-ham toastie) – these are a few themes around which Belgian festivals are based.

Although pre-Lenten Carnival provides the main excuse for mayhem to strike the streets of otherwise sober-sided towns and villages, there is scarcely a week of the year when a festival is not being held somewhere. The aim is to celebrate the past, keep tradition alive, and – oh yes, have a high old time.

CARNIVAL

Eupen's *Rosenmontag* procession (February) is a seemingly endless procession of floats, and marchers in a bewildering variety of costumes. Binche,

Procession of the Holy Blood, Bruges

an otherwise unremarkable town near Charleroi, has probably the most remarkable carnival (February).

Other towns have developed a gallery of characters that almost equal those of Binche's *Gilles*. Stavelot has its *Blanc-Moussis* (March) with their all-white costumes and long red noses; Fosse-la-Ville boasts the hunchbacked *Chinels* (March).

RELIGIOUS

The Basilica of the Holy Blood in Bruges contains a rock-crystal phial that is said to hold a relic of Christ's blood (see page 66). Every year it is carried around the city in the Biblical pageant called the Procession of the Holy Blood (May).

Veurne (see page 75) also takes its Bible seriously, in the Procession of the Penitents, when marchers clad in brown Capuchin habits carry crosses through the streets (July). The procession began in 1650 to make amends for the sacrilege of a soldier who had burnt the Holy Eucharist.

TRADITION

One great thing about tradition is that people often have no idea why certain festivals exist. Ypres' *Kattestoet* (Cat-

FOLKLORE DATES

February: Carnival Aalst; Gilles' Carnival, Binche; Carnival, Eupen; Carnival, Hasselt; Carnival, Malmédy.
March: Chinels' Carnival, Fosse-la-Ville; Dead Rat's Ball, Oostende; Carnival, Stavelot.
May: Procession of the Holy Blood, Bruges; Cat-throwing Festival, Ypres (even-numbered years only).
June: Re-enactment of the Battle of Waterloo (not every year).
July: Ommegang, Brussels; Procession of the Penitents, Veurne.
August: Planting the Meiboom (Tree of Joy), Brussels.
September: Procession of the Plague, Tournai.
October: Procession of the Pilgrims, Lier.

Kattestoet, or Cat-throwing Festival, Ypres

throwing Festival) falls, literally, into this category, as cats are thrown from the windows of the Cloth Hall (see page 74). Until 1870, they threw live cats; now stuffed toys take flight instead (May, alternate years).

No such uncertainty exists about Brussels' *Ommegang* (Procession) which re-creates the fabulous procession welcoming Emperor Charles V to Brussels in 1549. Only participants wearing 16th-century costume are allowed to take part in the performance. Some 1,200 of them represent members of the imperial family and court, the aristocracy, magistrates, guildsmen, soldiers and citizenry (July).

THE *GILLES* OF BINCHE

Carnival begins early in Binche. At 5 o'clock on a cold February morning, in houses throughout the town, *Gilles* are being dressed in their red, yellow and black costumes, with shoulder and collar ruffs, and with straw stuffed inside. Melodic piping and drumming announces that other *Gilles* (only males can be *Gilles*) have arrived. Stamping around on clogs is followed by a glass or two of champagne, and then the group goes off to round up more *Gilles*.

Soon the streets echo to the wail and beat of dozens of bands and the rhythmic stamping of clogs with bells on, all converging on the square outside Binche station. The noise, colour and sheer press of people are astonishing. Later, the *Gilles* put on identical masks and ostrich-plume head-dresses and dance to the Grand-Place, to be presented to the mayor. Thought to recall the Emperor Charles V's conquest of the Incas, the Carnival of Binche is unforgettable.

Children

Children are well catered for in Belgium, with a wide variety of museums, theme parks (see pages 156–7) and outdoor pursuits to keep the young and energetic busy.

MUSEUMS
These museums are likely to be of special interest to children.

Antwerpse Miniatuurstad (Antwerp Miniature City)
Children's tours of a sound-and-light show, combined with miniature buildings, that tells the story of how Antwerp grew as a city.
Hangar 15a, Cockerillkaai-Scheldekaaien, Antwerp (tel: (03) 237 0329). Open: daily 10am–6pm. Admission charge. Riverside.

Musée des Enfants/Kindermuseum (Children's Museum)
Exhibitions and displays on the changing patterns of children's lives in Belgium and abroad.
Rue du Bourgmestre/Burgmeestersstraat 15, Brussels (tel: (02) 640 0107. Open: weekends, Wednesday and school holidays, 2.30–5.30pm. Admission charge. Ixelles/Elsene.

Musée du Jouet/Speelgoedmuseum (Toy Museum)
Historical toys and other aspects of children's lives in the past.
Rue de l'Association/Verenigingsstraat 24, Brussels (tel: (02) 219 6168). Open: daily 10am–6pm. Admission charge. Metro: Madou.

Musée du Jouet (Toy Museum)
Displays some 1,000-odd toys of all kinds dating from the end of the 19th century to the 1950s.
Route de Lognoûle 6, Ferrières (tel: (086) 400198). Open: weekends and school holidays, 2.30–5.30pm. Admission charge. Ferrières is 9km west from Exit 48 on the E25 south of Liège.

Musée des Sciences Naturelles/Instituut van Natuurwetenschappen (Natural History Museum)
Enough dinosaur skeletons, dioramas of prehistoric life and displays of the natural world to fill the imagination of any child.
Chaussée de Wavre 260, Ixelles, Brussels (tel: (02) 627 4252). Open: Tuesday to Saturday 9.30am–4.45pm; Sunday 9.30am–6pm, closed Monday. Admission charge. Leopold District rail station.

Musée du Transport Urbain/Museum voor Stedelijk Vervoer (Public Transport Museum)
Vintage horse-drawn and electric trams are on show at this fascinating museum. When it is open, some of the electric trams run between the museum and the Royal Museum of Central Africa (see page 40).
Avenue de Tervuren/Tervurenlaan 364b, Woluwe-Saint-Pierre, Brussels (tel: (02) 515 3108). Open: first Saturday in April to first Sunday in October, weekends and public holidays only, 1.30–7pm. Admission and excursion charge. Tram 39 or 44 from Metro: Montgomery.

Speelgoedmuseum Mechelen (Mechelen Toy Museum)

Belgium's finest toy museum, with an enormous collection of historic toys.
Nekkerspoel 21, Mechelen (tel: (015) 557075). Open: Tuesday to Sunday 10am–5pm. Admission charge. Near Mechelen Nekkerspoel railway station.

NATURE PARKS

Places where children can get close to nature and rural life in a safe environment.

Crête des Cerfs (Stags' Crest)

A wooded nature park with fawns, hinds, does and other animals roaming in relative freedom. There is also a children's playground.
Bouillon (tel: (061) 467149). Open: daily 9am–sunset. Admission charge. Located 1km out of town.

Ferme de Dry Hamptay (Dry Hamptay Farm)

One of the popular attractions at Han-sur-Lesse (see pages 96–7), the farm includes a children's playground and an audio-visual projection of the chambers and galleries which cannot be visited in the Han caves.
Rue des Grottes 46, Han-sur-Lesse (tel: (084) 378231). Open: mid-March to beginning November, daily 12.30–5.30pm; July and August, noon–7.30pm. Admission charge. The farm is between the village and the Caves of Han.

Flindertuin (Butterfly Garden)

Situated adjacent to the Zwin Nature Reserve (see pages 72–3), this is a charmed garden with a 425sq m glasshouse filled with colourful and exotic butterflies.
Bronlaan 14, Knokke–Heist (tel: (050) 610472). Open: Easter to beginning October, daily 10am–5.30pm. Admission charge.

Walibi amusement park is no place for the faint-hearted

OTHER ATTRACTIONS

There are numerous attractions listed in other parts of this book which, while not designed exclusively for young children, are likely to appeal strongly to them. See, for example:
Antwerp Zoo (page 58);
Autoworld and the Belgian Comic Strip Centre (page 39);
Bokrijk Open-air Museum (page 76);
Euro Space Center (page 96);
Mini-Europe (page 28).

THEME PARKS

Belgians have a fondness for children's theme parks, and there seems to be no end to their number.

Adventure

These are more in the form of amusement parks.

Aqualibi

Associated with Walibi adventure park (see opposite), this tropical-ocean wonderland retains a year-round temperature of 29°C. Swimmers can descend a 140m flume, or relax on the wave-rippled beach.

Wavre (tel: (010) 414466). Open: April to September, daily 10am–6pm for visitors to Walibi only, 6–11pm for anyone; October to March, Wednesday to Friday 2–11pm and weekends 10am–11pm. Admission

Fun for all the children at Telecoo amusement park

charge. Exit 6 from E411 Brussels–Namur motorway; also signposted from Wavre railway station.

Bellewaerde

Located on an estate outside Ypres, in what was the tortured landscape of World War I (see pages 90–1), Bellewaerde now resounds to the excited cries of children.

Meenseweg 497, Ypres (tel: (057) 468686). Open: beginning April to beginning September, daily 10am–6pm (July and August, 9.30am–7pm); September to mid-October on weekends only, 10am–6pm. Admission charge. Located 6km outside Ypres on the N8.

Bobbejaanland

Named after its owner, the Cowboy and Western fan Bobbejaan Schoepen, this is a classic adventure park, in the Kempen (see pages 76–7). As well as thrills-and-spills rides, there is a floor-show and a

scaled-down Mississippi Riverboat, following the Western theme.
Lichtaart (tel: (014) 557811). Open: beginning April to mid-October, daily 10am–6pm (high season 9.30am–7pm); October, Friday to Sunday 10am–6pm. Admission charge. Exit 20 from E313.

Meli-Park
The attractions in this seaside park, including the rides and exhibits, are based on the theme of the 'honey bee'.
De Pannelaan 68, Adinkerke–De Panne (tel: (058) 420202). Open: 1 April to beginning September, daily 10.30am–5.30pm. Admission charge. By bus from Coast Tram terminal at De Panne (see pages 84–5).

Océade/Oceadium
A tropical-style-adventure pool, similar to Aqualibi, in Brussels' Bruparck centre (see pages 28–9).

Recreatiepark Zoet Water (Sweet Water Recreation Park)
Specialises in small children, with mini-cars, a miniature train, playground, 'Tarzan route', splash-pool, forest museum, etc.
Noësstraat 15, Oud-Heverlee (tel: (016) 477555). Open: April to September, Monday to Saturday 10am–7pm, Sunday 10am–8pm. Admission charge: October to March, weekends only 1–5pm. Admission free. Located 6km south of Leuven.

Telecoo
An amusement park set in marvellously scenic countryside along the River Amblève in the Ardennes (see page 99).

Walibi
An outstanding amusement park near

Brussels, the kind of place that gets the adrenalin flowing in kids aged from six to 60. Walibi's attractions include the Colorado Mine Tour; Dream World, which takes you through the land of 1001 Nights; and the thrills and spills of descending the Radja River.
Wavre (tel: (010) 414466). Open: April to August, daily and September weekends only 10am–6pm. Admission charge. Exit 6 from E411 Brussels–Namur motorway; also signposted from Wavre railway station.

EDUCATIONAL
These include safari parks and dolphinariums.

Dierenpark Planckendael (Planckendael Wildlife Park)
Not far from Brussels, this wildlife park brings together more than 1,000 animals in an open country setting.
Leuvensesteenweg 582, Muizen–Mechelen (tel: (015) 414921). Open: summer season, daily 9am–6.30pm; winter season, 9am–5pm. Admission charge. Located 5km from Mechelen on the N26.

Monde Sauvage Safari (Wild Safari World)
This park in the Ardennes hills is organized in several sections. The part where wild animals such as lions, tigers, jaguars, kangaroos, polar bears and wolves can be seen is accessible by car or on a special motorised train. Another part can be toured on foot, and this is where 'homelier' species like goats, donkeys and ponies are kept.
Fange de Deigné 3, Deigné–Aywaille (tel: (041) 609070). Open: 15 March to 15 November, daily 10am–7pm. Admission charge. Exit 45 from the E25 motorway south of Liège, then on the N678 and N666 for 10km.

Sports (participant)

*B*elgians share many of the same sporting interests as other nationalities, but there are some differences. Golf is not really widespread, with only around 50 courses in the country, although it is growing fast in popularity, while cycling is a sport that arouses strong passions and also gets masses of people on their bikes at weekends and vacation time.

CYCLING

Any trip to the countryside is sure to be livened by packs of racing cyclists whirring past in bright lycra blurs. Flanders is mostly flat, with both the coastal plain and the Kempen offering smooth roads under broad skies, but the lack of shelter from the wind means that cycling on level ground is not necessarily easy. Wallonia has the hills, and both along the River Meuse valley and in the Ardennes there are routes to challenge the best.

It is not necessary to practise racing or endurance to enjoy the experience, however. Bikes are available for hire from more than 50 railway stations, while mountain bikes are widely available for hire in the Ardennes.
Cycling information: The Belgian National Tourist Office and the provincial tourist offices publish brochures about cycling (see page 189 for addresses and telephone numbers); also from the Ligue Vélocipédique Belge/Koninklijke Belgische Wielrijdersbond (Belgian Cycling League), Avenue du Globe/Globelaan 49, B-1180 Brussels (tel: (02) 349 1911).

GOLF

Its far-from-extensive nature in Belgium may be related more to a shortage of facilities than to lack of interest. This situation is now being remedied, with practice and full-scale courses increasing in number. Most of them are adequately challenging, and there are several Open-standard courses.

A few clubs are strictly private, but at most it is possible for visitors to play, either by taking out temporary membership or by paying for each game.

Ardennes area
Durbuy Golf Club, Route d'Oppagne, Barvaux (tel: (086) 214454). An 18-hole course in a beautiful part of the Ardennes.

Royal Hautes Fagnes Golf Club, Balmoral, Spa (tel: (087) 771613). An 18-hole course just outside the famous mineral springs resort (see pages 98 and 126–7).

Brussels area
Royal Waterloo Golf Club, Vieux Chemin de Wavre 50, Ohain (tel: (02) 633 1850). One of the best, with 18-hole and 9-hole courses, restaurant, driving range, pro-shop, club hire, etc.

Royal Tervuren Golf Club, Kasteel Ravenstein, Tervuren (tel: (02) 767 5801). Similar facilities to the Royal Waterloo.

The Coast
Royal Zoute Golf Club, Caddiespad 14, Knokke–Zoute (tel: (050) 601287). A fine 18-hole course.

Keeping your eye on the ball can be difficult in this canoe-borne version of water polo

Golf information: Fédération Royale Belge de Golf/Koninklijk Belgisch Golf Federatie (Royal Belgian Golf Federation), *Chemin de Baudemont 23, 1400 Nivelles (tel: (067) 219525).*

SAILING

In addition to the extensive facilities at the coast for yachting, power-boating and windsurfing, the river and canal network and numerous lakes and recreation parks also offer sailing possibilities.

Sailing information: Verbond van Vlaamse Watersportverenigingen (Union of Flemish Watersport Foundations), *Beatrijslaan 25, 2050 Antwerp (tel: (03) 219 6967).*

HORSE-RIDING

The different characteristics of the Flemish and Walloon countryside make for a different horse-riding experience in each area, and riding is popular and widely available in both. Brussels, too, has extensive horse-riding facilities, particularly in the area around La Hulpe and the Forêt de Soignes/Zoniënwoud (Soignes Forest).

Horse-riding information: Fédération Royale Belge des Sports Equestres/ Koninklijke Belgische Ruitersport Federatie (Royal Belgian Federation of Equestrian Sports), *Avenue Houba de Strooper/Houba de Strooperlaan 156, B-1020 Brussels (tel: (02) 478 5056).*

TENNIS

A very popular sport, with many private and public tennis courts, both indoor and open-air, existing all over the country. In the Brussels area alone, there are more than 30 clubs.

Tennis information: Fédération Royale Tennis/Koninklijke Tennisbond (Royal Tennis Federation), *Galérie Porte de Louise, Louizaport 203, B-1050 Brussels (tel: (02) 513 2927).*

Sports (spectator)

*B*elgians are generally interested in the same kind of sports as people in neighbouring countries. Soccer is a firm favourite, for example, but there are a number of popular sports which lie somewhere between participant and spectator events, archery being one.

ARCHERY

Not horizontal archery usually, but vertical, tracing its origins to besieged cities where archers practised by firing into the air so as not to waste ammunition (presumably the enemy were out of range). Some parks have vertical archery rigs, from which marksmen compete to pick off brightly coloured targets; Josaphat Park in Brussels is one such (see page 33).

ATHLETICS

The Ivo Van Damme Memorial, named for a Belgian Olympic silver-medal winner who was killed in a road accident, takes place in August at Brussels' Heysel Stadium. It is one of international athletics' prestige meetings, attracting many top track and field competitors.

CYCLING

The name of Belgian champion Eddy Merckx, known as 'the Cannibal' for the way he ate up mountains, roads and competitors, is indelibly linked with cycling. Each spring, his lessons are relearned in hard-fought competitions like the Toer van Vlaanderen (Tour of Flanders) and the Flèche Wallonne (Walloon Arrow). The Tour of Belgium is in August, followed by the Eddy Merckx Grand Prix in September. All you need is a place at the roadside.

HORSE-BALL

This sport is of fairly recent origin and is a combination of handball and polo, with horses supplying the muscle-power and the players trying to score goals with a ball of leather thongs. A league has been formed and exhibition matches are played at special events such as the Libramont Agricultural Fair (see page 145).

Horse-Ball information:

Fédération Belge de Horse-Ball/Belgische Horse-Ball Federatie (Belgian Horse-Ball Federation), *Rue Belle-Vue/Bellevuestraat 14, B-1050 Brussels (tel: (02) 647 9297).*

HORSE-RACING

A sport that is undergoing a resurgence in interest; trotting meetings also take place. The Brussels area has not just one *hippodrome/renbaan* (racecourse), but three. These are: **Boitsfort/Bosvoorde**, Chaussée de la Hulpe/ Terhulpse-steenweg 51, Watermael Boitsfort/ Watermaal–Bosvoorde (tel: (02) 672 1484);

Hurtling through the Ardennes on the Spa-Francorchamps circuit

Groenendaal, Sint-Jansberglaan 4, Hoeilaart (tel: (02) 657 4186); **Sterrebeek**, Du Roy de Blicquylaan 43, Sterrebeek (tel: (02) 767 3591). Another course, in a superb seaside setting, is the **Wellington**, Prinses Stefanieplein 41, Oostende (tel: (059) 803636).

FOOTBALL
Also called soccer; *foot* in French; *voetbal* in Flemish. In **FC Anderlecht** (Avenue Theo Verbeeck 2, Brussels (tel: (02) 522 1539), Brussels has one of Europe's crack footballing squads, a team that is nearly always in contention when honours are at stake. **FC Bruges** (tel: (050) 386691) and **Standard Liège** (tel: (041) 522122) are generally not far behind.

International matches are played at the new **Heysel Stadium** beside the Bruparck recreation centre (see pages 28–9) and the national team's performances are generally creditable, but not enough to scale the footballing heights.

GOLF
A competition like the Belgian Classic, played at the Royal Tervuren Golf Club (see page 158), attracts great interest.

MOTOR SPORT
Belgium has two Fomula One-class racing circuits, one in Wallonia and the other in Flanders, which generally take turn-about to stage the Belgian Grand Prix, as well as hosting other motor and motorcycle competitions.

Spa-Francorchamps is not only one of the most testing, but also one of the most scenic circuits in the world, winding through the Ardennes hills and forests on a surface which is partly on public roads. **Heusden-Zolder** in the Kempen near Hasselt may be less visually dramatic, but the action is equally high-tension.

TENNIS
The Belgian Open and the Antwerp Classic (the winner gets a diamond-studded racquet) are the premier events.

Food and Drink

Master-chef Pierre Wynants does the honours at Brussels' 3-Michelin Star Comme Chez Soi

Belgian cuisine

Food is a passion in this country, which has more Michelin star restaurants per capita than France. Belgian cuisine is based on the country's own regional traditions: roots that can be taken quite literally in the case of Flemish asparagus, chicory (Belgian endive) from Brabant, even the humble Brussels sprout.

Herring, lightly salted on the boats, is eaten raw as *maatjes* at the coast and is a particular delicacy in the spring. Sole makes its appearance as *sole à l'Ostendaise*. North Sea shrimps are considered the finest tasting of all, and at Oostduinkerke some fishermen still catch them from the backs of sturdy horses (see page 73).

Other traditional Flemish fish dishes are *waterzooi op Gentse wijze*, a fish stew

originating in Ghent (although nowadays chicken is more often used than fish) and *paling in 't groen*, eel served in a grass-green sauce. Flanders has more than sea, however: its pigs, for example, might be interested to know that they will one day form a vital ingredient of Italy's Parma ham.

Brussels and Wallonia would not like it to be thought that they were a millimetre behind Flanders in the culinary stakes. A tradition in Brussels is cooking with the traditional local beers like *gueuze* and *faro*, and great steaming pots of Zeeland mussels have a fanatical following in Brussels – in fact, throughout Belgium.

Liège has given its name to *salade liègeoise*, a mixture of smoked bacon, potatoes, onion, parsley and French beans, and also to *ragoût liègois*, a simple stew of potatoes, vegetables and veal.

Jambon d'Ardennes (Ardennes ham), Ardennes pâtés and river trout have gained considerable renown. Autumn, and the game season in the Ardennes, is eagerly awaited, especially by followers of the 'weekend gastronomique' tradition when a weekend break is accompanied by wild boar, venison, hare or wildfowl.

An entire book could be devoted to Belgian cheeses, more than 300 varieties of them, each with a committed local following, but often, sadly, little known outside Belgium. Cheeses like Corsendonk, Passendale, Maredsous, Petrus, Château d'Arville, Wynendale, Rubens and Le Regalou are craftsman's cheeses, bearing no relationship to any mass-produced product.

It can be seen from this brief introduction that Belgium's cuisine is not only regional but unpretentious. It used to be easier to eat this way at a friend's house than in a restaurant, but times are changing; some of the select fraternity of Belgian master chefs have been instrumental in putting regional cuisine where it belongs – on the plate.

When all is said and done, there is always the Belgian *frite*, a speciality of Wallonia that has been exported to Flanders as the *friet*, to Britain as the chip, and to the world as the misnamed French fry.

Chocolates with instant allure

CHOCOLATES

Belgian *chocolatiers* (chocolate shops) glitter like jewellery stores, and many people rate their wares much more highly than mere precious stones. It is no exaggeration to say that the finest Belgian chocolates are devilish, addictive and ought to be sold with a government health warning.

Handmade pralines made by companies like Wittamer, Nihoul, Neuhaus, Godiva and Leonidas are the top of the range in taste and cost. They are sold loose, in bags weighing as little as 100g, or in boxes that range upwards to 2kg and more.

They come in a wide range of types, and rather than take a prepared box you should simply point to the ones you fancy tasting, or ask the shop assistant to create a representative mixture.

Such quality pralines are usually made with real cream and do not keep well – but they'll likely be gone long before shelf-life becomes relevant.

WHERE TO EAT

In the restaurant listings below, the following symbols have been used to indicate the average cost per person, not including alcohol.

F = BF600–BF1,000
FF = BF1,000–BF1,500
FFF = BF1,500–BF2,500
FFFF = more than BF2,500

BRUSSELS

This is a city where eating is taken seriously and quality is not an optional extra. There is a truly enormous number of restaurants covering a wide range of nationalities.

Belgian Food
Comme Chez Soi FFFF
Three Michelin stars and Belgium's most highly rated chef, Pierre Wynants. Advance reservations essential. Closed Sunday and Monday.
Place Rouppe/Rouppeplein 23 (tel: (02) 512 2921). Metro: Anneessens.
De l'Ogenblik FF
Heavenly taste in Parisienne bistro-style ambience. Closed Sunday.
Galerie des Princes/Prinsengalerij 1 (tel: (02) 514 5597). Galeries Royales Saint-Hubert/Koninklijke Sint-Hubertus Galerijen.
Marmiton FF
High standard at a modest price.
Rue des Bouchers/Beenhouwersstraat 43a (tel: (02) 511 7910). Ilot Sacré.
La Mirabelle F
Good-value restaurant popular with students.
Chaussée de Boondael/Boondaalse

Steenweg 459 (tel: (02) 649 5173). Near Université Libre de Bruxelles (Brussels Free University).
Quincaillerie FF
Trendy but good restaurant located in a former hardware store.
Rue du Page/Edelknaapstraat 45 (tel: (02) 538 2553). Ixelles/Elsene.
Scheltema FF
Good service and fine atmosphere complement seafood specialities. Closed Sunday.
Rue des Dominicains/Predikherenstraat 7 (tel: (02) 512 2084). Ilot Sacré.
La Sirène d'Or FFF
Seafood specialities beside Brussels' fish market. Closed Sunday and Monday.
Place Sainte-Catherine/Sint-Katelijneplein 1a (tel: (02) 513 5198). Marché-aux-Poissons/Vismarkt.
La Truite d'Argent FF
An outdoor terrace in good weather, and seafood specialities.
Quai aux Bois à Brûler/Brandhoutkaai 23 (tel: (02) 219 9546). Marché-aux-Poissons/Vismarkt.

Traditional Brussels
Au Vieux Bruxelles FF
A convivial 1880s-period restaurant specialising in mussels. Closed Sunday and Monday and public holidays.
Rue Saint-Boniface/Sint-Bonifaasstraat 35 (tel: (02) 513 0181). Metro: Porte de Namur/Naamsepoort.
In 't Spinnekopke F
Among Brussels' oldest restaurants, and serves many

ILOT SACRÉ

The 'stomach of Brussels' is a sight worth seeing for its colourful atmosphere, although many people dismiss it as a tourist trap. A few restaurants in the Ilot Sacré, or close by, which are worth visiting are Scheltema, Marmiton and De l'Ogenblik.

In some others it is wise to be wary if inexpensive menu items are 'not available' but the waiter can 'propose' you 'something special'; be sure that service and value added tax are included in the price and that two dishes are not being delivered when one would be adequate; be certain of the exact price of anything ordered, including house wine, aperitifs, etc.

traditional beer-sauce-based dishes. Closed Sunday and public holidays.
Place du Jardin-aux-Fleurs/ Bloemenhofplein 1 (tel: (02) 511 8695). Near Place Sainte-Catherine/Sint-Katelijneplein.

Brasserie de la Roue d'Or FF
An excellent brasserie with art nouveau and Magritte-style decor. Closed August.
Rue des Chapeliers/Hoedenmakersstraat 26 (tel: (02) 514 2554). Near Grand-Place/ Grote Markt.

't Kelderke FF
Hearty Belgian fare served in an atmospheric cellar. Specialises (but not exclusively) in mussels.
Grand-Place/Grote Markt 15 (tel: (02) 513 7344).

Ethnic Food
Cambodge F
Light, airy decor and good Cambodian

cuisine.
Rue Washington/Washingtonstraat 77 (tel: (02) 537 7098). Ixelles/Elsene.

Karibu FF
A taste of Zaïre.
Chaussée de Wavre/Waversesteenweg 346 (tel: (02) 230 3379). Southeast of centre.

Passage To India F
Unpretentious but high-quality Indian restaurant.
Chaussée de Louvain/Leuvensesteenweg 223 (tel: (02) 735 3147). North of centre.

La Porte des Indes FFF
Truly superb Indian cuisine, at a price. Closed Sunday lunchtime.
Avenue Louise/Louizalaan 455 (tel: (02) 647 8651 or 640 3059). Near Bois de la Cambre/Terkamerenbos.

American Food
Rick's Café Americain FF
A touch of Humphrey Bogart accompanies American and Mexican food.
Avenue Louise/Louizalaan 344 (tel: (02) 647 7530).

European Food
Paradiso
A hot-tip Italian restaurant, known only to insiders.
Rue Duquesnoy/Duquesnoystraat 34 (tel: (02) 512 5232).

FLANDERS

ANTWERP
Beluga FFF
Carries its maritime theme from the 1930s liner interior, via a beautiful view over the River Scheldt, to its seafood specialities.
Sint-Pietersvliet 3 (tel: (03) 226 1003).

De Mergpijp FF
One of those uniquely Antwerp kind of places: warm ambience, good food, and a haunt of artists as well as 'ordinary' people.
Vlaamsekaai 16 (tel: (03) 238 6197).

Falafel Beni F
One of the best places for tasting the Israeli/Lebanese snack called *falafel*, based on crushed deep-fried chickpeas.
Lange Leemstraat 188 (tel: (03) 234 2632).

Hollywood Witloof F
A curious but tasty blend of cafeteria style and old-cellar ambience.
Hofstraat 9 (tel: (03) 233 7331).

La Terrazza F
Straightforward, authentic Italian food.
Wisselstraat 2 (tel: (03) 226 6658).

Sir Anthony Van Dyck FF
Having relaunched in brasserie style, the Sir Anthony has lost its previous gravitas, but the food is still good and its location in the olde worlde Vlaeykensgang courtyard ensures that atmosphere remains.
Oude Koornmarkt 16 (tel: (03) 233 9125).

Panaché F
A reasonably priced delicatessen that packs taste into all it produces.
Statiestraat 17 (tel: (03) 232 6905).

BRUGES
Duc de Bourgogne FFF
Part of the medieval hotel of the same name, the restaurant is one of Bruges's famous places.
Huidenvettersplein 12 (tel: (050) 332038).

Kasteel Minnewater FF
Serves seafood specialities in a superb château overlooking an appropriately marine setting: the Minnewater canal. Closed Monday.
Minnewater 4 (tel: (050) 334254).

Koffieboontje F
A bright and cheerful restaurant concentrating on mussels and regional specialities.
Hallestraat 4 (tel: (050) 338027).

't Pandreitje FFF
Star quality Belgian cuisine in an ordinary-looking Bruges terrace house.
Pandreitje 6 (tel: (050) 331190).

Stove FF
Fine Belgian and French cuisine in a bistro-style restaurant. Closed Wednesday; also in summer Thursday lunch; in winter Tuesday evening.
Kleine Sint-Amandsstraat 4 (tel: (050) 337835).

Tanuki FF
Japanese specialities traditional-style, at surprisingly non-Japanese prices.
Noordstraat 3 (tel: (050) 347512).

Toermalijn FF
Hotel restaurant whose vegetarian cuisine puts meat and fish dishes in the shade.
Coupure 29 (tel: (050) 340194).

Food is a matter of proud display

THE COAST
Becassine FF
The chef achieves amazing culinary magic with prawns and other denizens of the deep, in a homey setting.
Rozenlaan 20, Oostduinkerke (tel: (058) 521100).

Old Fisher FF
Seafood specialities right where the fishing fleet lands its catch. The bouillabaisse is particularly fine. Closed Wednesday evening and Thursday.
Visserskaai 34, Oostende (tel: (059) 501768).

Ter Dijcken FFF
Fine restaurant with a wide range of menu possibilities, and with the accent on seafood.
Kalvekeetdijk 137, Knokke–Heist (tel: (050) 608023).

GHENT
Auberge de Fonteyne F
Typical Belgian cuisine in a hand-crafted art nouveau interior.
Gouden Leeuwplein 7 (tel: (09) 2254871).

Buddhasbelly F
As one might expect, Buddhasbelly serves excellent vegetarian cuisine that brings culinary enlightenment to all those who taste it. The prices are reasonable too.
Hoogpoort 30 (tel: (09) 225 1732).

Guido Meersschaut F
Owned by a local family who also have a fish-shop, the Guido Meersschaut restaurant naturally specialises in seafood in its Fish Market location. It is closed Sunday evenings and also on Mondays.
Kleine Vismarkt 3 (tel: (09) 223 5349).

Sint-Jorishof FFF
Just looking at this magnificent hotel-restaurant, which dates from 1228, is an event in itself. Its restaurant, overlooked by a balustraded balcony, serves Flemish and French cuisine. Closed Sunday evening.
Botermarkt 2 (tel: (09) 224 2424).

KEMPEN
Kasteel Sint-Paul FFFF
Something to save for a special occasion, because this particularly impressive country château is a bit off the beaten track, but its superb waterside setting and graceful ambience, plus carefully crafted French cuisine, together make for an extremely memorable experience.
Lagendalstraat 1, Lummen (tel: (013) 521809). Exit 26 from the A2 near Hasselt.

Kristoffel FFF
This fine restaurant conjures up the grace of a bygone era in its village location in the Kempen.
Dorpstraat 28, Bocholt (tel: (089) 471591).

WALLONIA

ARDENNES
Claire Fontaine FF
Uses the best of local produce in its engagingly traditional cuisine, served in a countryside restaurant beside the River Ourthe.
Route de Hotton 64, La Roche-en-Ardenne (tel: (084) 412470).

Les Falizes FF
A cosily tranquil dining-room in which to sample the finest Ardennes specialities.
Rue de France 90, Rochefort (tel: (084) 211282).

Sanglier des Ardennes FFF
One of the truly heavenly experiences in this beautiful area. Specialises in fish dishes, and game during the hunting season.
Rue Comte d'Ursel 99, Durbuy (tel: (086) 213262).

EAST CANTONS
Alte Herrlichkeit F
Traditional German–Belgian cooking in an old-style restaurant.
Gospertstrasse 104, Eupen (tel: (087) 552038).

Pip-Margraff FF
Something of an East Cantons institution, the Pip-Margraff delivers on the promise of good cooking. Closed Monday.
Hauptstrasse 7, Sankt-Vith (tel: (080) 228663).

Val de l'Our FF
Ardennes specialities for a moderate price in one of the prettiest parts of the country.
Rue du Village 150, Burg-Reuland (tel: (080) 329009).

GENVAL
Le Trèfle à Quatre FFFF
Restaurant of the Château du Lac hotel beside Genval Lake (see page 48), and a memorable eating as well as visual experience. Closed Monday and Tuesday.
Avenue du Lac 87 (tel: (02) 654 0798).

Shangri-la du Lac FF
A fine Chinese restaurant with an excellent view over Genval Lake.
Avenue du Lac 96 (tel: (02) 654 1244).

LIEGE
Au Vieux Liège FFF
Top-flight Belgian and French cuisine. Closed Sunday, also Wednesday evenings.
Quai de la Goffe 41 (tel: (041) 237748).

Chez Max FFF
Unpretentious, cosy restaurant that presents unbeatable Belgian cuisine.
Place de la République Française 12 (tel: (041) 220859).

Fiacre FF
Excellent-value regular cuisine served in a 16th-century ambience. Closed evenings of Monday, Tuesday and Wednesday.
Place Saint-Denis 2 (tel: (041) 231545).

Mamé Vî Cou FF
Walloon dialect for 'A Nice Old Lady', the oak-beamed restaurant focuses on Liège's own lip-smacking culinary traditions: pigs' kidneys flamed in *geneva*, chicken in beer, hot black pudding in acid cherries. Closed Monday.
Rue de la Wache 9 (tel: (041) 237181).

MEUSE VALLEY

Auberge de Bouvignes FFF

Top-rated farmhouse-style restaurant on
the banks of the River Meuse near
Dinant.
_Rue Fétis 112, Dinant–Bouvignes
(tel: (082) 611600)._

Château des Comtes F

Part of the works at Namur's Citadel
have been put to good use in this
inexpensive cellar restaurant which
concentrates on local dishes.
_Route Merveilleuse 50, Namur-Citadelle
(tel: (081) 222212)._

Château de Namur FFF

A castle that is frequently besieged on
account of its quality and elegant
surroundings.
_Avenue de l'Ermitage 1 (tel: (081)
742630)._

Prince de Liège FF

Moderately priced, considering the
excellent food which includes seafood
and Belgian specialities.
_Chaussée de Namur 96b, Gembloux
(tel: (081) 611244)._

SPA

Chalet du Parc F

Cheap 'n' cheerful tavern in the Parc de
Sept Heures (Seven O'Clock Park).
Parc de Sept Heures 1 (tel: (087) 772284).

Fontaine du Tonnelet FF

An elegant Italian restaurant, in the style
of a Tuscan villa, located beside the
red- and-white pavilion of the Fontaine
du Tonnelet (Tonnelet Spring).
Route du Tonnelet 82 (tel: (087) 772603).

Géronstère F

A fine, reasonably priced stone-built
country restaurant beside the Fontaine
de la Géronstère (Géronstère
Spring).
_Rue de la Géronstère 119 (tel: (087)
770372)._

Sauvenière FF

This excellent country restaurant
is situated next to the Fontaine de
la Sauvenière and Fontaine de
Groesbeeck (Sauvenière and Groesbeeck
Springs).
_Route de la Sauvenière 116 (tel: (087)
775168)._

The warm glow of appreciation reaches both
inside and out

TOURNAI

Charles-Quint FF

Art deco interior in a traditional Tournai
building, where French-style cuisine is
served. Closed Wednesday evening and
Thursday.
Grand-Place 3 (tel: (069) 221441).

Thieulerie FF

A fine local restaurant in the unlikely
surroundings of Tournai's medieval
Pont des Trous (Bridge of Holes)
overlooking the River Escaut (Scheldt).
Pont des Trous (tel: (069) 211616).

CAFES

With more than 400 different kinds of beer to choose from, each with its own unique glass, it is scarcely surprising that Belgians are fond of their cafés. They are a kind of home from home, as familiar as people's own living rooms. It is no exaggeration to say that all Belgian life is there.

ANTWERP
In Den Engel
A marvellously warm, friendly and atmospheric old café on Antwerp's Grote Markt, looking out on to the cobblestones and gabled guild-houses of the square. The city's own De Koninck beer is served here with due respect.
Grote Markt 3.

De Vagant
A specialist in *jenever/genièvre (geneva)* to which devotees come from all over to taste one of the 150 varieties on the menu.
Reijndersstraat 25.

Groote Witte Arend
Located in an old abbey, this 17th-century café is one of Antwerp's most intriguing, and customers drink to the sounds of classical music.
Reyndersstraat 12–18.

Kulminator
Should the beers in all of Antwerp's other cafés seem to offer an inadequate choice, the Kulminator may be the answer, with 550 beers on its menu.
Vleminckveld 32.

Pelgrom
A brick-walled cellar café that is brightly lit by candle-power and with various chambers and alcoves where customers sit at wooden benches.
Pelgrimstraat 15.

BRUGES
't Brugs Beertje
A popular, traditional café with 250 beers on its menu.
Kemelstraat 5.

BRUSSELS
A La Mort Subite
Stained-glass motifs, old photographs, paintings and prints on the walls; plain wooden chairs and tables. Specialities are traditional Brussels beers: *gueuze*, *faro* and *kriek*, as well as Trappist brews like Chimay, Maredsous and Grimbergen.
Rue Montagne-aux-Herbes Potagères/ Warmoesberg 7.

Archiduc
Its clientele may tend a little towards the painfully chic, but its fashion is state of the art.
Rue Antoine Dansaert/Antoine Dansaertstraat 6.

Au Bon Vieux Temps
Strong beer like Duvel is a firm favourite in this gloomily atmospheric old café.
Rue du Marché-aux-Herbes/Grasmarkt 12.

Cerceuil
Serenaded by funereal music, customers with a taste for the macabre sit at a coffin-lid table and drink beer from a pitcher in the form of a human skull.
Rue des Harengs/Haringstraat 10.

Cirio
Attracts a somewhat elderly and respectable clientele.
Rue de la Bourse/Beursstraat.

De Ultieme Hallucinatie
Art nouveau design and an extensive range of Belgian beers are just two reasons for visiting this characterful café.
Rue Royale/Koningsstraat 316.

Falstaff
Opened in 1904, Falstaff has added a touch of art deco to its art nouveau origins, while its waiters have acquired a reputation for arrogance which is not entirely deserved, although customers are expected to be suitably respectful.
Rue Henri Maus/Henri Mausstraat 17.

GHENT
't Dreupelkot
A characterful old café beside the River Leie, specialising in *geneva* and with a vast range of varieties.
Groentenmarkt 12.

Galgenhuisje
Students make this tiniest of cafés a lively and convivial place and a Ghent classic.
Groentemarkt 5.

Tolhuisje
The Little Toll House was once precisely that, being part of the infrastructure of Ghent's Renaissance-period harbour. Now it is a small and characteristic café.
Graslei 10.

Dulle Griet
Order a Kwak beer (see page 172) and you must deposit a shoe as guarantee for the valuable wooden framework without which a Kwak glass cannot stand – the theory being that shoeless customers will not escape with the frame.
Vrijdagmarkt 50.

LIEGE
Pierre Levée
Students find the cellar atmosphere (and perhaps also the 600 or so beers on offer) much to their liking.
Rue de Serbië 62.

Vaudrée II
The almost 1,000 beers that the café offers must surely form some kind of record, and with 24-hour opening there is time enough to sample all of them.
Rue Saint-Gilles 149.

is known only to a few.

Each has a distinct glass, some of them creations of sensuous beauty in themselves. You can tell what everyone in a bar is drinking just by the shape of their glass.

Brussels beers such as *gueuze*, *kriek* and *faro* are brewed from wheat and barley, fermented without yeast, and often have cherries or other fruit added. A *gueuze* like Mort Subite (Sudden Death) is sold in a champagne-style glass. A foamy *kriek* like Belle-Vue is a popular summer drink. Antwerp has its much-loved De Koninck, a copper-coloured, yeasty beer served in a *bolleke* (little ball); no visit to Antwerp would be complete without a taste.

Duvel (Devil) is a golden, potent refermented brew served in a glass whose well-endowed curves make it

Each individual type of beer is served in its own style of glass

BELGIAN BEER

The range and quality of Belgian beers is apt to stagger – often quite literally – beer-imbibing visitors. Michael Jackson, the world authority on beer (not the singer!), has described Belgium as the 'land of beer' and his book *The Great Beers of Belgium* goes a long way towards explaining why.

As does a startling statistic: there are more than 400 kinds of beer made in Belgium, a country of just 10 million people. A few are *pils* (lager) beers, like Stella Artois, Jupiler, Maes, Primus and Eupener, ordinary beers that people order as a *chope/pintje* (glass). The vast majority, however, are local beers, specialities of the region, city, town or even village; others are made by monks; several are so specialised that their secret easier to grip after drinking two or three. Kwak is served in the oddest glass of all, a scaled-down yard of ale with a slim bulbous base, which can only stand with the aid of a wooden support (which might also be said of anyone who drinks too many). Looking into a wide-wide-brimmed, 1-litre glass of La Lunette is like looking into an ornamental pool filled with beer.

An entire range of light beers called *blanche/witte* (white) beers have an appreciative following. Wheat-based, honey-coloured, cloudy and slightly bittersweet, they are often served with a slice of lemon and make a refreshing drink in warm weather. Both Flanders and Wallonia produce white beers, with Hoegaarden, Dentergems and Blanche de Namur being among the most popular.

Belgian monks have for centuries had a special interest where beer is concerned. Beers like Maredsous, Chimay, Orval and Grimbergen have a heavenly quality that is an intrinsic ingredient of the brew.

Finally, if you have ever been told that beer is the Forbidden Fruit, you can go right ahead and order one – a *Verboden Vrucht*.

GENIÈVRE/JENEVER (GENEVA)

Although the French and Flemish words translate into English as 'gin', this is not an adequate description of a drink which is very different from English gin and would not be seen dead in a cocktail. The old word *geneva* is more accurate.

Called a *witteke* in Flanders and a *pèkèt* in Wallonia, this stiff grain spirit is served in brimful glasses, some not much bigger than a thimble. Unlike Holland, where it is mass-produced in a few brands, Belgium has more than 270 brands produced by 70 distilleries,

each one with its own distinct flavour.

They range from a 'low' of around 30 per cent alcohol to above 40 per cent and some are flavoured with juniper, coriander and other herbs and spices. Among the interesting brands are Filliers Oude Graanjenever, De Poldenaar Oude Antwerpsche, Heinrich Pèkèt de la Piconette, Sint-Pol, and Van Damme. Those sold in stone bottles make ideal gifts.

A few specialist cafés serve only *genevas*, and Hasselt, a centre of production, boasts the National Geneva Museum (see page 76).

Hotels and Accommodation

Belgium subscribes to the official Benelux hotel classification system, which incorporates five star-ratings and two letter-ratings. The category into which a hotel falls is marked on a blue badge at the entrance to the hotel. Beginning at the low end, the categories are:

O: accommodation only, with guaranteed minimum standard of comfort, hygiene and safety;
H: very plain hotel, with moderate standard of comfort and facilities, with at least one bathroom per ten rooms;
1-star: plain, washstand in every room, breakfast available;
2-star: average, with bath/WC in at least 25 per cent of rooms, baggage-handling and food and drink available;
3-star: very good, with lift if more than two floors, food and drink available;
4-star: first class, with lift, in-room breakfast available, telephone and television in room;
5-star: luxury hotel, meets highest standard of comfort, amenities and service, *à la carte* restaurant.

Room rates and room features must be indicated on a list at reception and posted in the rooms; rates are inclusive of VAT and service charge. High season is 1 July to 31 August, plus the Easter, Whitsun, Christmas and New Year holiday periods. Most hotels offer special rates for children.

BRUSSELS

Brussels has all the facilities to be expected in a major city, and many hotels are in the process of upgrading their facilities to a level appropriate for

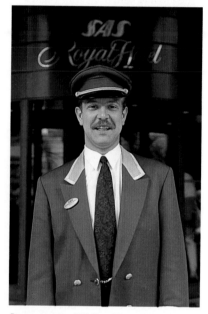

Doorman at the SAS Royal Hotel, Brussels

the 'Capital of Europe'.

In addition to city-centre locations, there are several 'satellite' areas: Avenue Louise/Louizalaan and Porte de Namur/Naamsepoort; near the World Trade Center; and Boulevard de la Woluwe/Woluwelaan. Ixelles/Elsene commune just south of the centre has many fine town houses which have been turned into hotels. The atmospheric Place Sainte-Catherine/Sint Katelijneplein area is another interesting option.

BUSINESS HOTELS

The biggest proportion of Brussels' hotel use is in the business sector. One consequence is that weekends are quiet, and business-oriented hotels try to attract leisure visitors with promotions and discounts. It is worth asking about reduced rates at weekends.

BRUSSELS ENVIRONS

There are few possibilities in the immediate surroundings. Staying outside can also present the problem of negotiating Brussels' awful rush-hour traffic, so a cost-benefit analysis must include more than the price in francs.

ACCOMMODATION CATEGORIES
Prices

Rates are usually based on bed-and-breakfast or on room-only rates per person. It is rare to have full board or half board, and anyway Brussels boasts a near-infinite variety of restaurants.

Deluxe ($250 plus)

Hotels in this category would include the Conrad Hilton, Carrefour de l'Europe, SAS Royal and Amigo – whose name is not Spanish but Brussels slang for a prison! Some have a special attraction which adds to their interest: the SAS Royal, for example, incorporates a section of the old city wall.

Premier ($150–$250)

The best of this category includes two splendid old hotels: the belle époque Pullman Astoria and French Renaissance-style Métropole, which both maintain the graces of pre-Euro Brussels. Beside Lac de Genval (Genval Lake, see page 48), the elegant Château du Lac is based on the design of an old abbey.

The neon-lit New Hotel Siru, Brussels

Moderate ($75–$150)

The choice in this extensive category is likely to depend on convenience. An interesting possibility is New Hotel Siru – not that it is any better than many others per se, but each room is 'decorated' with a painting or sculpture by a modern Belgian artist, some of international repute. The Albert Premier is a traditional old Brussels hotel.

Budget ($30–$75)

This kind of hotel is found in abundance around Ixelles/Elsene and Place Sainte-Catherine/Sint-Katelijneplaats. Les Bluets, a characterful old family-run hotel, and the Welcome, owned by a youthful entrepreneur and with a good seafood restaurant attached, are just two of the many possibilities.

Thermae Palace Hotel, Ostende

OTHER CITIES AND TOWNS

Cities like Antwerp, Ghent and Liège have similar facilities to Brussels, with prices tending to be less than in the capital (although not universally so). Bruges is a special case, with constant pressure on its hotel space, particularly in summer.

Towns like Tournai, Tongeren, Namur and Dinant have fewer hotels, yet are popular for historic or scenic reasons. As always, it is best to book in advance, but some kind of hotel space is almost certain to be available even at peak times. The exception is during special events, such as the Formula One Grand Prix at Spa–Francorchamps.

THE ARDENNES

As a rural vacation area, the Ardennes offer all forms of accommodation, from a tent in the forest to a deluxe hotel. Many people prefer farmhouse, cottage or chalet accommodation, believing (correctly) that it is closer to the traditional lifestyle of this historic and scenic region.

Hotels also have their place, however, and in the Ardennes you can find your own little 'gem', tucked away in a village or in a roadside clearing among the forests. 'Gastronomic weekends' are popular in the Ardennes, but the cuisine there is invariably superb at any time of the week, or year.

In addition to the reservation services listed below, accommodation in the Ardennes can be booked through: Belsud Reservations, Rue du Marché-aux-Herbes/Grasmarkt 61, B-1000 Brussels (tel: (02) 504 0390).

THE COAST

The range of hotels at the coast is enormous, and tends to be more individual than in the cities. There is everything from family-owned, converted townhouses to giant blocks,

CAMPING AND CARAVAN PARKS IN BELGIUM

These are popular activities throughout Belgium, but particularly in such areas as the Ardennes and the Kempen and at the coast. Especially popular are the Holiday Villages (French, *Villages de Vacances*; Flemish, *Vakantiedorpen*; German, *Feriendörfer*).

Facilities range from small grounds with fairly basic services for campers, to Provincial Recreation Areas and campsites with chalets, tent and caravan zones, restaurants, bars, swimming-pools, beaches, amusement centres, cycle-hire and other entertainments.

The provincial tourist authorities (see page 190) publish brochures listing the camping and caravan parks in their area. At peak times in the most popular areas it is advisable to book in advance.

and with all possible permutations in between.

In some resorts, the seafront is lined with hotel and apartment blocks, which gives convenient access to the beach but may not be restful or have much in the way of 'character'. Conversely, some of the more individual hotels are further from the beach, a fact which may be important if travelling with small children.

OTHER TYPES OF ACCOMMODATION

Youth hostels ($10–$18)

There are youth hostels all over Belgium, with facilities ranging from basic dormitory accommodation and shared showers to double rooms with en-suite showers.

Youth hostel information: Les Auberges de Jeunesse, Rue Van Oost/Van Ooststraat 52, B-1030 Brussels, (tel: (02) 215 3100); Vlaamse Jeugdherbergcentrale, Van Stralenstraat 40, B-2060 Antwerp (tel: (03) 232 7218).

Bed and Breakfast (B&B) ($20–$30)

It is possible to stay as a paying guest with a local family, or in ordinary bed-and-breakfast accommodation, the latter being effectively the same thing but more often made available by householders as much for financial as for cultural reasons.

Bed and Breakfast information: provincial tourist offices (see page 190) and local tourist offices. Also from Taxistop, Place de l'Université 41, B-1348 Louvain-la-Neuve (tel: (010) 451414).

RESERVATIONS

Hotel and other accommodation in Belgium can be arranged by Thomas Cook Network locations, travel agents, Belgian Tourist Offices in your home country, local tourist offices in Belgium, and by Belgium Tourist Reservations, Boulevard Anspach/Anspachlaan 111/box 4, B-1000 Brussels (tel: (02) 513 7484).

This youth hostel, which forms part of a world-wide network, is open to all travellers, regardless of race, religion or political opinions, on presentation of a valid youth hostel membership card.

On Business

*D*espite their reputation for enjoying a 'Burgundian lifestyle', Belgians are no laid-back bons-vivants when it comes to business. One fact should be borne in mind when doing business in Belgium: this country is the European Union's biggest exporter on a per capita basis and the methods used to achieve such success should not be underestimated.

BRUSSELS: EURO-CITY

Among the business and diplomatic bodies based in Brussels are: the Association of European Airlines, Eurocontrol (European Air Traffic Control Organization), Federation of European Community Savings Banks, International Customs Co-operation Council, North Atlantic Assembly, NATO (North Atlantic Treaty Organization), SWIFT (Society for Worldwide Interbank Financial Telecommunication), UNICE (European Union of Industrial and Employers' Confederations).

CONVENTIONS AND EXHIBITIONS

Brussels

The city is a busy venue, particularly the Exhibitions Park at the Heysel, but also several other locations.

For further information, contact: Les Pyramides, Place Rogierplaats 2b, B-1210 Brussels (tel: (02) 203 3283). Parc des Expositions de Bruxelles/Tentoonstellingspark van Brussel, Place Belgique/Belgiëplein, B-1020 Brussels (tel: (02) 477 0263). Palais des Congrès/Paleis voor Congressen, Coudenberg 3, B-1000 Brussels (tel: (02) 513 4130).

General

Antwerp, Ghent, Kortrijk and Liège have important conference and exhibition centres, or are well known for a particular event.

For further information, contact: Belgium Convention and Incentive Bureau (BECIB), Rue du Marché-aux-Herbes/Grasmarkt 61, B-1000 Brussels (tel: (02) 513 2721).

ETIQUETTE

This varies depending on the nature of the business, but in general business people behave formally and expect punctuality and traditional dress style in their business acquaintances. This is softened by the ritual of hand-shaking with men, and kissing the cheeks of closer women colleagues.

Invitations to Belgians' homes for dinner are not handed out lightly, and should be treated accordingly.

FINANCE

The Foreign Private Investment Bureau of the Ministry of Economic Affairs (see Useful Addresses, opposite) provides information and advice on financial incentives available for foreign businessmen and/or companies interested in setting up an operation in Belgium.

There are four stock exchanges, with the vast majority of transactions being carried out at the Brussels exchange. Other exchanges are in Antwerp, Liège and Ghent. For information, contact: Commission de la Bourse de Bruxelles/

Beurscommissie van Brussel, Palais de la Bourse/Beurspaleis, B-1000 Brussels (tel: (02) 511 1362).

LAW

Differing rules may apply to EU and non-EU citizens wishing to work, invest or do business in Belgium. Depending on the nature of the enquiry, further information can be obtained from the Belgian embassy or consulate in an individual's own country; the commercial attaché at the embassy of one's own country in Belgium; or national or local chambers of commerce in Belgium.

OPENING HOURS
Offices

Offices are usually open 8.30am–5.30pm, with 30 minutes or an hour for lunch, although many people work longer hours. They close at the same time on Friday, but many office-workers try to get away early on Friday.

TAXATION

Questions concerning Value Added Tax (VAT), both regulations and registration, should be addressed to TVA Enregistrement et Domaines/BTW Registratie en Domeinen, Cité Administrative de l'Etat/Rijksadministratief Stad, Tours des Finances/Financiën Toren, Boulevard du Jardin Botanique/Kruidtuinlaan 50, boîte/bus 39, B-1010 Brussels. (tel: (02) 210 2611).

USEFUL ADDRESSES
Chambers of Commerce

American Chamber of Commerce, Rue E Clausstraat 17, B-1050 Brussels (tel: (02) 647 5801).
Antwerp Chamber of Commerce, Markgravestraat 12, B-2000 Antwerp (tel: (03) 232 2219).
Belgian/Canadian Chamber of Commerce, Avenue de la Sapinière/Dennenboslaan 23, B-1180 Brussels (tel: (02) 375 8229).
British Chamber of Commerce, Avenue Col-Vert, Groenkraaglaan 1, B-1170 Brussels (tel: (02) 678 4792).
Brussels Chamber of Commerce, Avenue Louise/Louizalaan 500, B-1050 Brussels (tel: (02) 648 5002).
Charleroi Chamber of Commerce, Boulevard Général Michel 1a, B-6000 Charleroi (tel: (071) 321160).

Government

Belgian External Trade Office, World Trade Center, Boulevard Emile Jacqmain/Emile Jacqmainlaan 162 (tel: (02) 206 3511). This official promotion office publishes details of business opportunities in its regular bulletins.
Ministry of Economic Affairs, Square de Meeûs 23, B-1040 Brussels (tel: (02) 506 5111).

The European Parliament, Brussels

Practical Guide

Contents

ARRIVING
Entry formalities
European Union (EU) citizens do not require a passport but should have an identity card or other proof of identity; for UK citizens this means a British passport. Citizens of all other countries require a passport.

Visas
Citizens of most European countries, the USA, Australia, New Zealand, Canada, Japan and some other countries do not require a visa, except for stays of more than three months; all others will need visas.

By air
Brussels National Airport at Zaventem, 14km from the city, is the country's international airport. The usual facilities are available, but not all are on a 24-hour basis. A frequent train service links the airport with Brussels, journey time 20 minutes. The (very slow) bus BZ operates between Brussels centre and the airport, while the Belgian airline Sabena operates express coaches to and from Antwerp. Taxis are plentiful but not cheap and 'unofficial' taxis also operate.

A few international flights, from London and Amsterdam, land at Antwerp, Liège or Ostend.

Airport tax is included in the price of the air ticket, not paid separately. For flight inquiries (tel: (02) 722 3111).

By boat
Belgium has extensive car ferry and jetfoil connections with Britain. Oostende and Zeebrugge are the terminals for services from London, Ramsgate, Felixstowe and Hull.

By car
From Paris to Brussels on the E19 is

310km, from Amsterdam 232km; from Oostende and Zeebrugge on the E40 is 114km, from Cologne 228km.

By train

Oostende, Zeebrugge, Antwerp, Brussels and Liège are important points on the European rail network. Regular services connect with Paris, Amsterdam, Berlin, Milan, Copenhagen, Basle and various East European capitals, with the Eurostar (Channel Tunnel) service from London, and with ferries from Britain. Details of services, including night trains, can be obtained from the *Thomas Cook European Timetable*.

CAMPING, see page 177.

CHILDREN

Facilities for children are similar to those found in any developed country (see pages 154–7). Admission charges to museums and other attractions are usually at reduced rates for children.

CLIMATE

The climate is temperate, with the best weather between April and October. July and August can be quite hot, but rain is probable even then. Winters range from mild to severe, although temperatures rarely fall below freezing for long.

Average summer temperature is 19°C; in winter 3°C; peaks and lows show a much wider spread, with summer temperatures into the mid-30s and winter often below freezing.

CRIME

Crime is not a major worry, although it does exist, mainly in the form of petty theft from cars and of handbags and wallets. Take the usual precautions and do not leave items on car seats where

they can be spotted and the car broken into. Violent offences are rare. Drugs-related crime is on the increase.

CUSTOMS REGULATIONS

Travellers arriving from within the EU need not complete Customs formalities. Travellers from a non-EU country must complete Customs formalities in the usual way. No further tax is payable on goods purchased for personal use, including gifts, in another EU country.

The following are some guide levels for personal use (travellers may need to prove that excess is for personal use): 800 cigarettes, 400 cigarillos, 200 cigars, 1kg tobacco; 90 litres wine; 10 litres spirits; 20 litres intermediate products such as sherry and port.

Citizens of non-EU countries: 200 cigarettes or 50 cigars or 250g tobacco; 2 litres still wine; 1 litre spirits or 2 litres sparkling or fortified wine; 50g perfume and 0.25 litres eau de toilette.

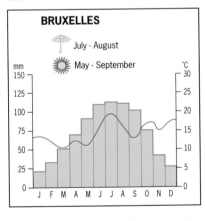

BRUXELLES

☂ July - August
☀ May - September

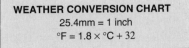

WEATHER CONVERSION CHART
25.4mm = 1 inch
°F = 1.8 × °C + 32

Conversion Table

FROM	TO	MULTIPLY BY
Inches	Centimetres	2.54
Feet	Metres	0.3048
Yards	Metres	0.9144
Miles	Kilometres	1.6090
Acres	Hectares	0.4047
Gallons	Litres	4.5460
Ounces	Grams	28.35
Pounds	Grams	453.6
Pounds	Kilograms	0.4536
Tons	Tonnes	1.0160

To convert back, for example from centimetres to inches, divide by the number in the third column.

Men's Suits

UK	36	38	40	42	44	46	48
Rest of Europe	46	48	50	52	54	56	58
US	36	38	40	42	44	46	48

Dress Sizes

UK	8	10	12	14	16	18
France	36	38	40	42	44	46
Italy	38	40	42	44	46	48
Rest of Europe	34	36	38	40	42	44
US	6	8	10	12	14	16

Men's Shirts

UK	14	14.5	15	15.5	16	16.5	17
Rest of Europe	36	37	38	39/40	41	42	43
US	14	14.5	15	15.5	16	16.5	17

Men's Shoes

UK	7	7.5	8.5		9.5	10.5	11
Rest of Europe	41	42	43		44	45	46
US	8	8.5	9.5	10.5	11.5	12	

Women's Shoes

UK	4.5	5	5.5	6	6.5	7
Rest of Europe	38	38	39	39	40	41
US	6	6.5	7	7.5	8	8.5

TRAVELLERS WITH DISABILITIES

Services and access for people with disabilities are nothing to be proud of, but the situation is improving. Some museums and public buildings have ramps for wheelchairs. Public transport is also a difficult proposition.

The French-speaking community publishes a guide, the *Guide Touristiques et de Loisirs,* containing much detailed information for travellers with disabilities; the Flemish provinces publish guides to their 'disabled-friendly' public services and places. Both are available from tourist offices (see page 189).

For further information, contact:

UK: Royal Association for Disability and Rehabilitation (RADAR), 25 Mortimer Street, London W1N 8AB (tel: 0171-637 5400).

US: Society for the Advancement of Travel for the Handicapped, 347 Fifth Avenue, New York, NY10016 (tel: 212/447 7284).

DRIVING

Documents

National driving licences are acceptable. Green Card insurance is required. Foreign-registered vehicles must display a nationality badge.

Practical

Fuel stations and garages are plentiful. Unleaded petrol and diesel are universally available, along with Super and Normal leaded petrol.

Breakdowns are handled by several motoring organisations, including Touring Secours/Wegenhulp (Touring Assistance). Emergency number (070) 344777.

Rental

The main international car-hire companies are represented and have desks at Brussels National Airport:

Avis (tel: (02) 730 6211).
Budget (tel: (02) 646 5130).
Europcar (tel: (02) 348 9212).
Hertz (tel: (02) 726 4950).

Roads

The *autoroute/snelweg* (motorway) network is excellent, but traffic gets bogged down at rush-hour and on city ring roads. Belgium has one of Europe's worst road accident records.

Driving in Belgium is on the right. A menace in urban areas is the 'priority from the right' system, whereby traffic coming from the right takes priority over traffic already on a road (except where that road is posted with orange-diamond signs). Trams have priority.

Rules

Speed limits are (unless otherwise posted): 50kph (31mph) in built-up areas, 90kph (55mph) on main roads and 120kph (75mph) on motorways.

Dipped headlights are mandatory after nightfall and in poor visibility – drivers of right-hand-drive vehicles must convert their headlights.

A fire-extinguisher and emergency triangle must be carried as well as driver's licence and vehicle registration papers.

Children under 12 are not allowed in front seats if there is room in the back of the vehicle. Safety belts must be worn in the front and back of vehicles.

ELECTRICITY

The unit of electricity is 220 volts AC (50 cycles). Sockets are for two-pin round plugs.

EMBASSIES

UK: Rue Arlon/Arlenstraat 85, Brussels (tel: (02) 287 6211).
USA: Boulevard du Régent/Regentlaan 27, Brussels (tel: (02) 508 2111).
Canada: Avenue de Tervuren/Tervurenlaan 2, Brussels (tel: (02) 741 0611).
Australia: Rue Guimard/Guimardstraat 6, Brussels (tel: (02) 231 0500).
New Zealand: Boulevard du Régent/Regentlaan 47, Brussels (tel: (02) 512 1040).

EMERGENCY TELEPHONE NUMBERS

Accidents: 100.
Police: 101.
Fire-service: 100.
Standby doctors: (02) 479 1818.
Standby dentists: (02) 428 9045.

MasterCard cardholders may use any Thomas Cook location to report loss or theft of their card and obtain an emergency replacement, as a free service.
Thomas Cook traveller's cheque refund (24-hour service; report loss or theft within 24 hours): tel: (0800) 1 2121 (toll-free).

HEALTH

There are no mandatory vaccination requirements. AIDS is present. Rabies is present in rural areas. Food and water are safe. UK travellers can obtain free or reduced-cost emergency medical treatment if they possess NHS form E111.

Belgian medical services are excellent, and many doctors speak English. Health advice can be obtained from your Thomas Cook travel consultant.

LANGUAGE

The three official languages are
French, Flemish and German. English
is widely spoken. Brussels is bi-lingual:
French and Dutch.

Numbers

English	French	Dutch	German
one	un, une	één	eins
two	deux	twee	zwei
three	trois	drie	drei
four	quatre	vier	vier
five	cinq	vijf	fünf
six	six	zes	zechs
seven	sept	zeven	sieben
eight	huit	acht	acht
nine	neuf	negen	neun
ten	dix	tien	zehn

Days of the week

English	French	Dutch	German
Monday	Lundi	Maandag	Montag
Tuesday	Mardi	Dinsdag	Dienstag
Wednesday	Mercredi	Woensdag	Mittwoch
Thursday	Jeudi	Donderdag	Donnerstag
Friday	Vendredi	Vrijdag	Freitag
Saturday	Samedi	Zaterdag	Samstag
Sunday	Dimanche	Zondag	Sonntag

Basic words and phrases

English	French	Dutch	German
good morning	bonjour	goedemorgen	guten tag
good afternoon	bonjour	goedemiddag	guten tag
good evening	bon soir	goedenavond	guten abend
goodbye	au revoir	tot ziens	auf wiedersehen
please	s'il vous plaît	alstublieft	bitte
thank you	merci	dank u wel	danke schön
yes	oui	ja	ja
no	non	neen	nein
how much?	combien?	hoeveel?	wieviel?
excuse me	pardon	pardon	bitte
sorry	excusez-moi	pardon	tut mir leid

INSURANCE

You should take out personal travel insurance before leaving, from your travel agent, tour operator or insurance company. It should give adequate cover for medical expenses, loss and theft, personal liability (but liability arising from motor accidents is not usually included – see below) and cancellation expenses. Always read the conditions, any exclusions and details of cover, and check that the amount of cover is adequate.

If you hire a car, collision insurance, often called collision damager waiver or CDW, is normally offered by the hirer, and is usually compulsory. Check with your own motor insurers before you leave, as you may be covered by your normal policy. If not, CDW is payable locally and may be as much as 50 per cent of the hiring fee. Neither CDW nor your personal travel insurance will protect you for liability arising out of an accident in a hire car, eg if you damage another vehicle or injure someone. If you are likely to hire a car, you should obtain such extra cover, preferably from your travel agent or other insurer before departure.

If you are taking your own motor vehicle on holiday, check with your motoring insurers on your cover both for damage, loss and theft of the vehicle and for liability. A Green Card is recommended. It is also possible to buy packages providing extra cover for expenses resulting from breakdowns and accidents.

LOST PROPERTY

If missing property may have been stolen, report it to the police and get an officially stamped copy of your statement for insurance claims.

MAPS

Tourist offices have free maps and city plans. Bookshops sell maps.

MEDIA

There is a weekly English-language magazine, *The Bulletin*, and the *International Herald Tribune* and many British newspapers are widely available. *Le Soir* (French), *De Standard* (Dutch) and *Grenz-Echo* (German) are the best quality papers. For financial news, *De Financieel Economische Tijd* (Dutch) and *L'Echo* (French) are recommended.

MONEY MATTERS

Currency

The currency is the Belgian franc (BF). Notes are of 10,000, 2000, 1000, 500, 200 and 100 francs; coins 50, 20, 5, and 1 franc, and 50 centimes.

Credit cards and cheques

International credit and charge cards are widely accepted. Traveller's cheques can be exchanged for francs at banks, foreign exchange offices and many hotels, and can be used to settle bills in major hotels, restaurants and some shops. Eurocheques can be written for up to BF7,000 with a supporting Eurocheque card.

Cash machines

Automatic cash-dispensers ('Mister Cash' and 'Bancontact') are widely available, and accessible by some foreign Eurocheque, credit and charge cards.

Taxes

Many shops operate a tax-refund system for non-EU foreign visitors.

Currency exchanges

Banks and major foreign exchange traders often give the best rates. Small street booths and outlets at the airport and main railway stations tend to offer poor rates and charge high commissions.

Thomas Cook MasterCard traveller's cheques are safer than carrying large amounts of cash and in the event of loss or theft can quickly be refunded. Branches of Thomas Cook at the following locations will change currency and cash traveller's cheques (free of commission in the case of Thomas Cook MasterCard traveller's cheques). They offer 'Moneygram', a quick international money transfer service, and can also provide emergency assistance in the case of loss or theft of Thomas Cook MasterCard traveller's cheques:

Koningin Astridplein 33, Antwerp (tel: (03) 226 2953).

Grand-Place/Grote Markt 4, Brussels (tel: (02) 513 2845).

19 Rue de Bouchers/Beenhouwerstraat 19, Brussels (tel: 02) 511 01 50).

OPENING HOURS
Shops open Monday to Saturday, 9am–6pm; some close on Monday. There are few late-night shops, but the neighbourhood 'corner store' may stay open until 9pm. **Banks** are open 9am–4pm, with an hour for lunch.

ORGANISED TOURS
Chatterbus (individualistic guides): Rue des Thuyas/Thujastraat 12, Brussels (tel: (02) 673 1835).
De Boeck (throughout Belgium): Place de Brouckercplein 50, Brussels (tel: (02) 218 6898).
ARAU (architecture and history): Rue du Midi/Midistraat 2, Brussels (tel: (02) 513 4761).

PHARMACIES
A list of nearby out-of-hours pharmacies is posted at every pharmacy. Many items are prescription-only and there is often a relatively small range of freely available medicines. Supermarkets (open until 8pm) are other sources for items such as nappies and tampons. Condoms are sold in pharmacies only.

PLACES OF WORSHIP
Belgium is 90 per cent Catholic, and although that figure masks many non-practitioners, religion is still a powerful force, especially in country areas. Brussels and Antwerp have churches, mosques, synagogues and temples from many religions.

POLICE
There are two main police branches: the Police/Politie, ordinary local police; and the Gendarmerie/Rijkswacht, who handle serious crime. (See **Emergency Telephone Numbers**, page 183.)

POST OFFICES
Open Monday to Friday, 9am–4pm, with smaller offices closing noon–2pm. Some open on Saturday morning. In Brussels, the office at Gare du Midi/Zuidstation is open permanently. Post boxes are painted red.

PUBLIC HOLIDAYS

1 January	New Year
March/April	Easter Monday
1 May	Labour Day
May	Ascension Day
May/June	Whit Monday
21 July	National Day
15 August	Assumption
1 November	All Saints
11 November	Armistice Day
25 December	Christmas

PUBLIC TRANSPORT
Bus
Buses are not a good way to travel long distances – the train is faster. District

and regional services are better, particularly in the Ardennes and other areas where the train service is limited, although few out-of-season bus services run. Metropolitan and local services are adequate. Bus terminals are usually sited next to railway stations.

Metro/Tram

Brussels and Antwerp have fast and efficient, but not extensive, metro (underground) systems. Tram systems are more extensive, both in these cities and in Liège, Ghent, some other towns, and along the coast (see pages 84–5).

Tickets (for buses as well) are either single trip, called a direct/direkt, or multiple-trip tickets which must be cancelled in an onboard machine and are available from drivers or (better value) from stations. Day tickets may be the ideal choice for short-stay tourists; monthly and even yearly passes are also available, but require photographs and a visit to the issuing office.

Taxis

The tip is included in the fare, which by law has to be metered.
Antwerp: Antwerp-Taxi (tel: (03) 238 3838).
Brussels: Taxis Bleus (tel: (02) 268 0000); Taxis Verts (tel: (02) 349 4949).
Liège: Melkior (tel: (041) 522020).

Train

There is an extensive and efficient rail network, both internally and internationally. Internal services are of three types: Inter-City (IC), Inter-Regional (IR) and Local (L). Second-class weekend returns cost 40 per cent less than regular returns and are valid from noon Friday to noon Monday, but return cannot be made earlier than noon

Saturday. Tourrail cards give good-value unlimited travel for five days during a 17-day period. InterRail tickets valid for one month's travel on the European network are available, as are three types of Eurodomino ticket: for three, five or 10 days' travel in a single month. Full details of services can be obtained from the SNCB/NMBS timetable, the Indicateur/Spoorboekje.

For Train information:
SNCB/NMBS, Rue Ravenstein/Ravensteinstraat 60, Brussels (tel: (02) 203 3640).

For Belgium's national and international rail services and connections, consult the *Thomas Cook European Timetable*, published monthly and available from Thomas Cook branches in the UK and Belgium.

SENIOR CITIZENS

Some benefits apply to all senior citizens, others only to Belgians. Many museums, concert halls, theatres and other public and entertainment facilities (not cinemas) offer reduced-rate tickets. Some tour companies do likewise, but reduced-rate travel on trains and buses requires a Belgian identity card.

STUDENT AND YOUTH TRAVEL

Reduced-rate student and youth rail travel is available to students in possession of a valid student card and young people under 26. For information on youth hostels, see page 177.
There are reception services in Brussels for students and young travellers:
Acotra World, Rue de la Madeleine/Magdalenasteenweg 51, B-1000 Brussels (tel: (02) 512 8607).
Infor-Jeunes/Info-Jeugd, Rue du Marché-aux-Herbes/Grasmarkt 27, B-1000 Brussels (tel: (02) 426 3333).

TELEPHONES

Numbers

Telephone services are operated by Belgacom.

Country code 32.

Brussels city code (02); Antwerp (03); Bruges (050); Ghent (09); Liège (041). If phoning from abroad, delete the 0. To dial abroad 00 + country code + area code + subscriber number. UK 44; USA and Canada 1; Ireland 353; Australia 61; New Zealand 64. Information 1207/1307 (internal); 1204/1304 (international). Telegrams 1225/1325. Telexes and faxes 1235/1335.

Charges

Public telephones accept BF5 and BF20 coins, or BF200 and BF500 Telecards available from post offices, railway stations and news vendors. There are three price bands: zonal, inter-zonal and international. The cheapest calls are direct dial; operator-assisted and collect connections cost more. Calls from hotel rooms may well be in excess of the standard cost.

Reduced rates: Internal – Monday to Friday, 6.30pm–8am, weekends and public holidays all day; twice as long for the same price as full rate. International – Monday to Saturday 8pm–8am, Sunday all day; 25 per cent longer for the same price as full rate.

THOMAS COOK

The Thomas Cook bureaux de change listed on pages 185–6 can arrange guided city tours and sell city maps, Thomas Cook timetables and guidebooks, phonecards and travel insurance, as well as foreign currency and traveller's cheques.

TIME

Belgium is on Central European Standard Time: GMT plus 1 hour in winter and plus 2 hours in summer. For most of the year, Belgium is one hour ahead of the UK and Ireland, five hours ahead of US Eastern Standard Time, and 14 hours behind Australia (Sydney).

TIPPING

Taxis, most restaurants, hairdressers and some other businesses include a service charge in the bill. As a result, Belgians rarely do more than 'round up' the change. Ushers at some cinemas and theatres expect a small tip (a BF20 coin is adequate) for taking your ticket.

TOILETS

Attendants require a small payment: the amount is posted. In many cafés and restaurants, men's and women's toilets are only notionally separated.

TOURISM ADDRESSES

Belgium has an efficient tourist information network, with national, regional, provincial, city, district and local offices. In French-speaking areas, they are called Office du Tourisme or Syndicat

d'Initiative; in Flemish-speaking areas, VVV (Vereniging voor Vreemdelingen Verkeer); and in the German-speaking area, Verkehrsamt. In all bigger offices and many smaller ones, some staff will speak English.

The tourist office will provide both maps and information, as well as making hotel bookings, giving opening times, arranging visits and guided tours.

National

Flanders: Toerisme-Vlaanderen, Rue du Marché-aux-Herbes/Grasmarkt 61, B-1000 Brussels (tel: (02) 504 0390).
Wallonia: Office de Promotion du Tourisme, Rue du Marché-aux-Herbes 61, B-1000 Brussels (tel: (02) 504 0390).

Brussels

Tourist Information Brussels, Hôtel de Ville/Stadhuis, Grand-Place/Grote Markt, B-1000 Brussels (tel: (02) 513 8940).

Forêt de Soignes

Provinces

Antwerp: Karel Oomsstraat 11, B-2018 Antwerp (tel: (03) 216 2810).
East Flanders: Koningin Maria-Hendrikaplein 64, B-9000 Ghent (tel: (091) 221637).
Flemish Brabant: Vanderkelenstraat 30, 300 Leuven (tel: (016) 267620).
Hainaut: Rue des Clercs 31, B-7000 Mons (tel: (065) 360464).
Liège: Boulevard de la Sauvenière 77, B-4000 Liège (tel: (041) 224210).
Limburg: Universiteitslaan 1, B-3500 Hasselt (tel: (011) 237980).
Luxembourg: Quai de l'Ourthe 9, B-6980 La Roche-en-Ardenne (tel: (084) 411011).
Namur: Rue Pieds d'Alouette 18, Parc Industriel, B-5100 Naninne (tel: (081) 408010).
Walloon Brabant: Chaussée de Bruxelles 218, B-1410 Waterloo (tel: (02) 351 1200).
West Flanders: Kasteel Tillegem, B-8200 Bruges (tel: (050) 380296).

East Cantons

Mühlenbachstrasse 2, B-4780 Sankt-Vith (tel: (080) 227664).

WALKING AND HIKING

Some walking and hiking routes have been grouped under the heading 'long-distance pathways' by two associations, one in Flanders, the other in Wallonia.

For further information, contact: Grote Routepaden Lange Afstandswandelwegen, Van Stralenstraat 40, B-2008 Antwerp (tel: (03) 232 7218). Sentiers de Grandes Randonnées, Rue Katteput/Katteputstraat 26, 1000 Brussels (tel: (02) 465 3554).

ACKNOWLEDGEMENTS
The Automobile Association wishes to thank the following libraries and photographer for their assistance in the preparation of this book.

PICTURES COLOUR LIBRARY 69 Bruges canal; **REX FEATURES LTD** 16a King Albert II, 16b King Albert II and Queen Paola; **SPECTRUM COLOUR LIBRARY** 179 European Parliament
The remaining transparencies are held in the AA PHOTO LIBRARY and were taken by Alex Kouprianoff.

The Automobile Association would also like to thank Ms Brigitte Pinckaers of Thomas Cook, Brussels.

CONTRIBUTORS
Series adviser: Melissa Shales   **Copy editor**: Ron Hawkins   **Indexer**: Marie Lorimer   **Designer**: Design 73
Thanks also to George McDonald for his updating work on this revised edition